Classroom Bullying Prevention, Pre-K–4th Grade

Classroom Bullying Prevention, Pre-K–4th Grade Children's Books, Lesson Plans, and Activities

Melissa Allen Heath, Tina Taylor Dyches, and Mary Anne Prater

LINWORTH

AN IMPRINT OF ABC-CLIO, LLC
Santa Barbara, California • Denver, Colorado • Oxford, England

Copyright 2013 by ABC-CLIO, LLC

Library of Congress Cataloging-in-Publication Data

Heath, Melissa Allen.
  Classroom bullying prevention, pre-K-4th grade : children's books, lesson plans,
and activities / Melissa Allen Heath, Tina T. Dyches, and Mary Anne Prater.
      pages cm
  Includes bibliographical references and index.
  ISBN 978-1-61069-097-3 (pbk.) — ISBN 978-1-61069-098-0 (ebook) (print)
  1. Bullying in schools—Prevention.   I. Dyches, Tina Taylor.   II. Prater, Mary Anne.
III. Title.
  LB3013.3.H434 2013
  371.5'8—dc23   2012032960

ISBN: 978-1-61069-097-3
EISBN: 978-1-61069-098-0

17 16 15 14 13   1 2 3 4 5

This book is also available on the World Wide Web as an eBook.
Visit www.abc-clio.com for details.

Linworth
An Imprint of ABC-CLIO, LLC

ABC-CLIO, LLC
130 Cremona Drive, P.O. Box 1911
Santa Barbara, California 93116-1911

This book is printed on acid-free paper ∞
Manufactured in the United States of America

Copyright Acknowledgments

Book cover of *Chrysanthemum* copyright © 1991 by Kevin Henkes. Used by permission of HarperCollins Publishers.

Book covers from *I Get So Hungry* by Bebe Moore Campbell, illustrated by Amy Bates; *Stand Tall, Molly Lou Melon* by Patty Lovell, illustrated by David Catrow; *Be Good to Eddie Lee* by Virginia Fleming, illustrated by Floyd Cooper; *Keeping Up with Roo* by Sharlee Glenn, illustrated by Dan Andreasen; *Thank You, Mr. Falker* by Patricia Polacco; *Crow Boy* by Taro Yashima are all used by permission of Penguin Group (USA) Inc. All rights reserved.

Cover illustration copyright © 2002 by Laura Huliksa-Beith from *The Recess Queen* by Alexis O'Neill. Scholastic Inc./ Scholastic Press. Reprinted by permission.

Jacket design from *Yoon and the Jade Bracelet* by Helen Recorvits, pictures by Gabi Swiatkowska. Text copyright © 2008 by Helen Recorvits. Pictures copyright © 2008 by Gabi Swiatkowska. Reprinted by permission of Farrar, Straus and Giroux, LLC.

Book cover copyright © 2002 by Tricycle Press. Jacket illustration © 2002 by Glin Dibley, from *Don't Laugh at Me* by Steven Seskin and Allen Shamblin, illustrated by Glin Dibley. Used by permission of Tricycle Press, an imprint of Random House Children's Books, a division of Random House, Inc.

Contents

Introduction

The numbers and statistics describing bullying and the negative repercussions resulting from bullying are overwhelming. As educators, we must personally and collectively take a stand against bullying and prepare our students to do likewise. Rather than passively tolerating bullying, student bystanders must be mentored and encouraged to actively take a stand, step in, and speak up. "It's time to confront bullying, harassment, and violence whenever and wherever we find it. This can be our contribution. We can make a difference, both in classrooms and in the world" (Henkin, 2005, pp. 64–65).

To assist us in making this contribution, this book of ready-to-use lesson plans and activities addresses bullying prevention in elementary school classrooms (Pre-K–4th grade). In total, the book contains 20 lesson plans: Fifteen lesson plans are included in Chapter 3 and five lesson plans are included in Chapter 4. Each lesson plan is based on a bully-themed children's picture book and includes activities that "stretch" the story, actively involving students and applying core messages. Each prepared lesson plan requires minimal preparation and serves as a basic guide to help identify core ideas and teaching points.

Lesson plans provided in this book strengthen student bystander support against bullying. The stories and activities teach and encourage all students to follow three simple strategies: take a stand, step in, and speak up.

The primary audience of this book is community and school librarians and elementary school teachers serving Pre-K–4th-grade students. This includes general and special area teachers (e.g., art and music teachers, special education teachers, and paraprofessionals). Additionally, school-based mental health professionals—including school counselors, school psychologists, and school social workers—may also utilize this book's resources to teach social skills in classrooms and small group counseling sessions. Although school librarians, teachers, and school-based mental health professionals represent a variety of professions, for simplicity we refer to this combined group as "educators."

This book is not intended to be used in isolation as a singular strategy to end bullying. Recognizing the interrelated and complex factors that create bully-free environments, this book and the included lesson plans supplement schoolwide efforts to reduce and eliminate bullying. In particular, the selected stories and accompanying lesson plans are designed to help students understand the need for everyone to feel welcomed, valued, and respected.

In Chapter 1, "Bullies, Victims, and Bystanders," we build the case for classroom-based bibliotherapy. This short introductory chapter provides a quick overview of bullying and research-based prevention strategies. Additionally, we emphasize the importance of strengthening the anti-bullying power of bystanders, who represent the vast and often silent majority of students. To counter bullying, we also encourage educators to create and maintain a safe and caring classroom environment with clearly identified behavioral expectations.

Chapter 2, "Sharing Books with Our Students," includes a brief summary of implementing school-based bibliotherapy and reasons for student participation in such activities. Readers are guided through the process of reading and discussing carefully selected bully-themed children's literature with students. We emphasize the importance of initiating group discussions about bullying, friendship, kindness, and conflict resolution. By sharing stories with students, a common classroom language is established that supports a safe and caring learning environment. Following group discussion, students participate in activities that stretch each story's core message into action, solidifying learning with an applied activity. Across the school year, we encourage educators to frequently refer to examples, terms, and phrases from these stories and to continue teaching lessons that strengthen bystander support and target critical anti-bullying social skills.

Chapter 3, "Lesson Plans to Strengthen Bystander Support," builds on information presented in Chapters 1 and 2. Chapter 3 begins with an annotated list of 15 children's bully-themed picture books. Each book provides examples of how bystanders did or did not support others who were bullied. Following the annotated list, we provide lesson plans for each picture book. These lesson plans serve as a basic guide to (a) clearly identify each book's core messages and lesson objectives; (b) specify supplies and materials needed for associated classroom activities; (c) identify questions to promote group discussion (before and after reading the book); (d) list key vocabulary (new terms); and (e) outline activities, extending stories into practical application. Reproducible activity sheets and suggested activities accompany each lesson plan. We also encourage educators to carefully adapt lesson plans to better meet the unique needs of their students (e.g., cognitive ability, social/emotional maturity, culture, communication skills, and individual interests).

Similar to the previous chapter, Chapter 4, "Lesson Plans to Increase Support for Vulnerable Students," begins with an annotated list of selected picture books. Each of the five selected books is then included in a lesson plan with related activities and handouts. In this chapter, we place a special emphasis on the importance of bullying prevention with special populations. The books and activities in Chapter 4 stress the important responsibility of protecting individuals who are inherently more vulnerable to bullying. More specifically, picture books in this chapter focus on individuals with special needs, such as physical, educational, and emotional disabilities. Chapter 4 lesson plans help educators teach bystanders to better support and defend the rights of individuals with special needs, the importance of including *all* classmates, and the importance of treating others with respect, kindness, and sensitivity.

This book's Appendix A contains an annotated bibliography of additional bully-themed children's picture books. Educators may consider these books when recommending books to parents and children. These books may also be used to more specifically target specific student needs and situations related to bullying. The appendix also describes additional resources and educational materials for educators and parents. Each item is briefly described. These resources include Internet websites with useful information, brief articles, and educational materials and books.

Appendix B is a compilation of the key vocabulary words from the books and their corresponding lesson plans.

As a tool for educators to create and strengthen positive, supportive, and inclusive classroom environments, this book offers economical, school-friendly, prevention strategies. The purpose of this book—and the basic premise behind each lesson plan included in Chapters 3 and 4—is to channel students' positive energy into building supportive classroom environments and fortifying classroom rules that counter bullying. Responsibility is placed on bystanders to actively and responsibly become involved when they see or are aware of bullying and to take a stand, step in, and speak up. Each selected children's book and accompanying lesson plan builds bystander support and encourages inclusiveness for all students.

(1) Take a stand

I **take a stand** against bullying.

(2) Step in

I **step in** and protect those who are bullied.

(3) Speak up

I **speak up** when I see bullying.

Figure I.1. Three strategies to build bystander support.

Chapter 1

BULLIES, VICTIMS, AND BYSTANDERS

Remember your first reaction when you heard about the 1999 Columbine High School shooting? All of us, from those directly involved to those watching television news reports, were horrified. As details were released and the facts confirmed, questions surfaced: How could this have happened? Could something like this happen in my school?

Sadly, the majority of school shooters have something in common—a history of being bullied and rejected. Rage and anger fueled their violent revenge. They struck out at those who excluded them, ridiculed them, and acted unkindly toward them. A string of school shootings, including Columbine, led federal and state education agencies to mandate school-based bully prevention programs. More recently, following several high-profile suicides related to bullying, President Barak Obama voiced his concern, emphatically stating: "We've got to dispel the myth that bullying is just a normal rite of passage, or an inevitable part of growing up. It's not" (U.S. Department of Education, 2010).

Although representing a small portion of bullying's negative ramifications, high-profile incidents of suicide and school violence garner public attention and demand responsive action. On an individual basis, a bully's unkind acts and hurtful words are permanently etched into our memories. We do not want our own children and students to feel unsafe in our schools; to fear coming to school; to avoid using school restrooms; or to feel isolated, disconnected, and not included in our classrooms. We want bully-free classrooms, bully-free schools, bully-free communities, and a bully-free world. Although that is a tall order, we have power right now to bully-proof our classrooms. So let's get started!

What Is Bullying?

Every child remembers school bullies and victims. Children also remember those who stood by watching—the bystanders—and who said nothing to stop the bullying. For children, sometimes it is difficult to know when good-natured teasing crosses the line and becomes bullying. When teasing one another, children may poke fun at one another without anyone feeling hurt. In fact, underlying friendship is the basis from which good-natured teasing evolves. Table 1.1 identifies the differences between teasing and bullying.

Bullying occurs when one or more individuals (bullies) impose their power (physical, social, and/or intellectual) over one or more individuals (victims/targets) with the intent to gain control over, to embarrass, or to inflict harm or discomfort. Over time, bullies repeatedly pick on victims (Olweus, 1993). Three primary elements distinguish teasing from bullying: (a) imbalance of power, (b) personal pain (physical, emotional, or social), and (c) persistence over time. In summary, bullies attempt to gain *power* or control over victims; bullies cause *pain* either physically, emotionally, or socially; and bullies *persist* in these attempts. Figure 1.1 (The Three Ps of Bullying) illustrates these three elements that define bullying.

When bullying occurs, everyone suffers, including bullies, victims, and bystanders. Table 1.2 identifies key terms and definitions and describes how victims are affected by bullying. Bullying might be physical (hitting or pushing), verbal (name calling and teasing), or relational (excluding peers, telling stories to ruin reputations). Verbal and relational bullying may occur in direct person-to-person interactions or may be perpetrated electronically via cell phones or the Internet (e.g., Facebook, e-mail, instant messaging). This type of electronic bullying is called cyber bullying.

Table 1.1
Differences between Normal Scuffles and Bullying

Normal Scuffles	Bullying
Incidents happen occasionally and involve a variety of students	Incidents happen repeatedly, typically involving the same students (bully/bullies and victim/victims)
Harm is unintended	Harm is strategic and intended
Interactions are not malicious and do not entail serious physical and/or emotional harm	Verbal and/or physical threats to others often include threat of physical harm and/or emotional harm
All involved appear equally upset and angry	Bully appears calm and victim appears upset (victim is emotionally reactive)
Power and control do not appear to fuel the situation	Bully seeks control and power over victims
Motivation does not appear to be one person getting what he or she wants	A pattern of the bully manipulatively and purposefully getting what he or she wants
Person who inflicted harm is sorry and admits responsibility	Bully who inflicted harm appears uncaring, minimizes extent of harm, blames others, and avoids responsibility
Those involved are willing to make compromises and take steps to solve problems	Bully appears uninterested in compromising and taking steps to resolve problems

Where Does Bullying Occur?

Bullying occurs *everywhere*. However, bullying is perpetrated most frequently in toxic social environments, particularly in classrooms and schools that lack consistent and effective discipline. Most often, bullying occurs in places with minimal adult supervision, such as playgrounds, school buses, hallways, lunchrooms, and restrooms. Although less obvious to adults, bullying also occurs in classrooms (Parault, Davis, & Pelligrini, 2007). Additionally, students who have access to electronic devices such as cell phones and the Internet have few limits regarding when, where, or whom they bully (Willard, 2007). In fact, cyber bullying has become an increasingly hot topic in middle school and high school settings (Willard, 2007).

Students often report that teachers and other staff either do not notice, do not care, or choose to ignore bullying. Unfortunately educators with these attitudes and dispositions are unlikely to respond to bullying situations. In fact, students report that bullies intentionally stay "under the radar." Often in the presence of adults, bullies avoid adult attention by continually pestering victims in small ways (Coloroso, 2008). A bully's raised eyebrow, staring looks, swift glances, and intermittent hand and facial gestures are all controlling strategies intended to keep victims under constant emotional duress. Although these mean-spirited actions may occur outside the teacher's awareness, on-looking classmates understand this type of relentless control yet rarely step in to counter such behavior. Victims struggle not only with being bullied but with secondary victimization, knowing no one cares enough to get involved—to take a stand, step in, and speak up against bullying.

How Does Bullying Affect Students?

Adults and students often hold misperceptions about bullying. They may underestimate how and to what extent bullying affects others. Tables 1.3 and 1.4 clarify common misperceptions about bullying. In particular, adults often underestimate the extent and severity of bullying. When adults ignore and discount bullying behaviors, bullying escalates and schools take on an increasingly hostile environment.

Figure 1.1. The three Ps of bullying: power, pain, and persistence.

Table 1.2
Bullying: Related Terms, Types of Bullying, and Impact of Bullying

Term	Description
Roles in bullying	
• Bully	Student with power (social and/or physical) who repeatedly picks on another student or group of students with the intent to inflict harm or discomfort
• Victim	Student who is the target of bullying
• Bystander	Student who observes bullying—may ignore bullying, encourage bullying, or take a stand against bullying
Types of bullying	
• Physical bullying	Hitting, pushing, kicking, slapping, pinching, biting, poking, choking, tripping, stealing or damaging property
• Verbal bullying	Name calling, using slurs, ridiculing, insulting, teasing, mocking, threatening, insulting, intimidating, manipulating, terrorizing; in person or via electronic means (cyber bullying)
• Relational bullying	Excluding, rejecting, humiliating, and discounting peers; telling stories to ruin reputations; spreading rumors; in person or via electronic means (cyber bullying)
Impact on victims	
• Emotional	Fear and anxiety
	Depression
	Decreased self-esteem
	Frustration
	Anger
• Behavioral	Crying
	Withdrawal and school avoidance
	Aggressive behavior
	Lower academic achievement
	Difficulty making and keeping friends

From *Classroom Bullying Prevention, Pre-K–4th Grade: Children's Books, Lesson Plans, and Activities* by Melissa Allen Heath, Tina Taylor Dyches, and Mary Anne Prater. Santa Barbara, CA: Linworth. Copyright © 2013.

Table 1.3
Information for Adults: Facts Countering Common Misperceptions about Bullying

Misperceptions	Facts
Bullying toughens kids for the real world. It is a natural part of growing up.	Just because bullying is commonly experienced does not mean it is a normal part of growing up. There is nothing "natural" or "normal" about bullying. Bullying is not an acceptable behavior and should not be tolerated. Bullying does not toughen kids but rather reduces feelings of self-worth and increases feelings of fear and anxiety.
"Sticks and stones may break my bones but words will never harm me."	Mean-spirited comments hurt us emotionally. Tied to painful memories, verbal wounds last a lifetime.
Bullies lack social skills and are social misfits.	Although bullies lack empathy, bullies are often smart, socially adept, and popular.
Victims and bullies are two totally different groups of kids.	There is a huge overlap between the two groups: 75 percent of students who are bullied also bully others.
Boys are bullies and girls are victims.	All types of bullying are perpetrated by both boys and girls. Bullies target both genders.
Girls dominate relational bullying.	Although girls more frequently engage in verbal bullying than physical bullying, both genders use relational bullying to obtain and sustain power over others.
Some victims deserve to be bullied because their behavior and strong reactions bring it on themselves.	No one deserves to be bullied. Victims are *never* the cause of bullying behavior. The bully is responsible for bullying. Bystanders are also responsible when they encourage the bully or do not step in to stop bullying.
Students should not tell a teacher or another adult because "telling is tattling."	Reporting bullying to adults brings bullying into the open and reduces the bully's power. Adults must help students clearly differentiate between "tattling" and "telling." Students may need an anonymous way to report bullying and positive behaviors that deserve recognition. Teachers might designate an anonymous "classroom comment box." Anonymous reporting encourages students to report both good and bad behaviors, expanding teachers' awareness of student activity.

Table 1.4
Information for Students: Facts about Bullying

False	True
Bullying toughens kids up. It is part of growing up.	Just because bullying happens a lot does not mean it is OK. There is nothing "normal" about bullying. Bullying does not toughen kids. It makes kids feel awful about school and life.
"Sticks and stones may break my bones but words will never harm me."	Mean words hurt us. Mean words stick inside our brains and are hard to forget.
Bullies don't have friends.	Even though bullies don't think about others' feelings, they have friends who think bullying is funny and cool.
Bullies and kids who are bullied are two totally different types of kids.	Most kids who are bullied also bully others.
Boys are bullies and girls are victims.	Both boys and girls bully other kids. Both girls and boys get bullied.
Girls bully with unkind words and boys bully with hitting and shoving.	Both girls and boys say unkind words and use their power to keep some kids from joining their group. Boys might hit and shove more often, but some girls also hit and shove.
Some kids get what's coming to them because they are weak and strange.	No one should be bullied. It is *never* the victim's fault. The bully is responsible. If other kids join in with the bully, they share responsibility for bullying. Those who watch and don't do anything (bystanders) are not stopping bullies from hurting others. Bystanders are also part of the bullying.
Kids should not tell a teacher or another adult because "telling is tattling."	Telling an adult brings bullying into the open. Adults need to know about bullying so they can help stop it. "Tattling" and "telling" are not the same.

On a personal level, the effects of bullying are both immediate and long term. Victims typically suffer lower academic achievement, higher rates of depression, decreased self-esteem, and difficulties with interpersonal relationships across the life span (Nansel, Craig, Overpeck, Saluja, & Ruan, 2004). Bullying is also linked to victims' frustration, anger, and aggressive behavior (Nansel, Overpeck, Haynie, Ruan, & Scheidt, 2003). In addition to negative repercussions for victims, students who witness bullying are often fearful of bullies' power. They avoid intervening for fear of being victimized themselves.

How Can Schools Intervene and Prevent Bullying?

Reports of the effectiveness of schoolwide anti-bullying programs have been mixed. Some schoolwide prevention programs have demonstrated progress in reducing bullying. At the same time, large reviews of anti-bullying programs indicate minimal change in bullying over time (Merrell, Gueldern, Ross, & Isava, 2008). We should not, however, abandon the goal of reducing and eliminating bullying. As caring educators, we have power to support students and offset bullying's negative impact (Sprague & Walker, 2005). Figures 1.2 and 1.3 are helpful in visualizing bystander power. We can teach and routinely remind students about bystander power and its potential to offset and "shrink" bully power. It is also important for students to understand that if they ignore bullying, in effect they are actually supporting bullying.

Looking forward, our students will one day remember the kindness of adults who showed concern and stepped in to stop bullying. Students will also recall the bravery of peers who, rather than silently standing by, took action to stop bullying. Students will remember those who took a stand, stepped in, and spoke up.

Adults' Influence

Children's resilience is strengthened when they receive consistent social support from adults. Additionally, adults who visibly take a stand against bullying are positive role models. Our increased awareness of and intolerance for bullying is a critical component of anti-bullying efforts. In all our interactions—in all we say and do—we must model kindness and respect for each individual. We must closely monitor student interactions, taking the time and effort to step in and stop bullying behaviors. We must protect and befriend students who are victimized by bullying. Indifference—ignoring and discounting bullies' mean-spirited behavior—is unacceptable: We must model behavior that supports respect and safety for all students, laying the groundwork for inclusive and nurturing classroom environments.

Bystanders' Influence

Since most bullying occurs in the presence of multiple bystanders, we must encourage all adults, including parents, to empower bystanders in denouncing bullying. We must identify, implement, and consistently support clear rules and consequences that counter bullying behaviors. We must also provide support and direct supervision for all students and provide positive reinforcement and activities that build cooperative and pro-social behavior (Sprague & Walker, 2005).

Although at first glance bullying may appear to occur solely within the bully–victim dyad, it is important to look at the bigger picture—the social environment in which bullying develops and thrives (Parault et al., 2007). The focus of effective interventions must consider two important contributing factors: (a) students' and educators' calloused tolerance for and acceptance of bullying, and (b) insufficient and ineffective student problem-solving strategies to address bullying, particularly for victims and bystanders (Davis & Davis, 2007; Heath, Moulton, Dyches, Prater, & Brown, 2011). It is important to access the untapped power of bystanders, the silent majority who comprise 80 percent of the student population. This vast majority of students—those who are not bullies or victims—stand as observers on the perimeter of bullying (Davis & Davis, 2007). These reticent students must be prepared to take a stand against bullying, to actively step in, and to speak up. As educators, we are in an excellent position to coach, encourage, and strengthen bystander power.

Figure 1.2. Bully–victim dyad. When bystanders do not take a stand, step in, and speak up, bullies are powerful.

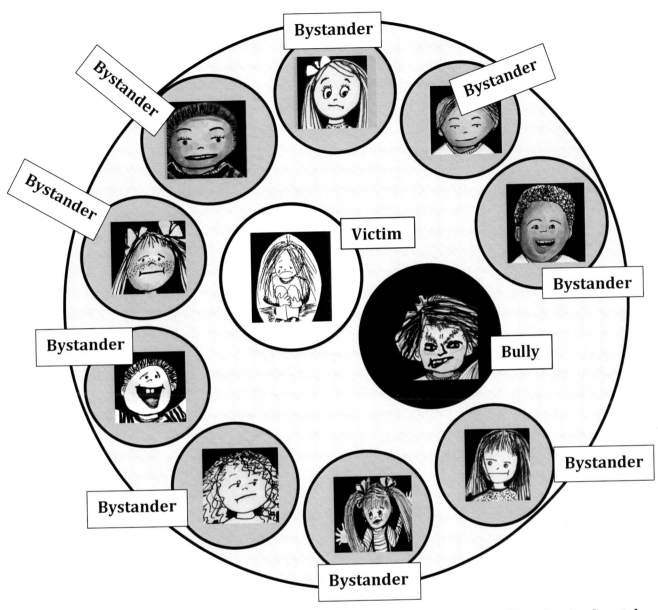

Figure 1.3. Bystanders, bully, and victim. Bystanders outnumber bullies. When bystanders take a stand, step in, and speak up, bullies shrink. Bystanders are more powerful than a bully.

As a tool to create and strengthen positive, supportive, and inclusive classroom environments, this book offers economical, school-friendly, bully prevention strategies. The purpose of this book—and the basic premise behind each lesson plan included in Chapters 3 and 4—is to channel students' positive energy into building supportive classroom environments and fortifying classroom rules that counter bullying. Responsibility is placed on bystanders to actively and responsibly become involved, to take a stand against bullying, to step forward, and to speak up against bullying. Each selected children's book and accompanying lesson plan builds bystander support and encourages inclusiveness for all students.

Chapter 2

SHARING BOOKS WITH OUR STUDENTS

Bibliotherapy is based on the premise that individuals have the capacity within themselves to solve personal problems, to move forward, and to heal. For centuries, stories, fables, and parables have passed treasured bits of wisdom from one generation to the next. When woven within an interesting plot and presented with colorful pictures and interesting characters, stories communicate strong messages to children. For children, rather than merely presenting facts and lecturing, a better option is to share a good story. Good stories hold interest and attention. Children enjoy and remember stories.

Optimally, stories create leverage to shift children's perceptions, which in turn lays the groundwork for changing emotions and challenging behaviors.

Carefully selected stories hold the power to introduce and model strategies to help children change thoughts, feelings, and behaviors. Based on principles of cognitive behavioral therapy (CBT) and play therapy, bibliotherapy is frequently used by counselors to address children's problematic thoughts and behaviors (Cohen, Mannarino, & Deblinger, 2006). Moving away from external control of behavior (e.g., rewards and punishment), CBT therapists propose that individuals change their behavior by changing underlying motivation, thoughts, perceptions, and attitudes. In regard to effectiveness, bibliotherapy has been successful in treating a variety of children's emotional and behavioral problems, such as anxiety (Rapee, Abbott, & Lyneham, 2006), depression (Stice, Rohde, Seeley, & Gau, 2008), aggression (Shechtman, 1999, 2000, 2006), and bullying (Teglasi, Rahill, & Rothman, 2007).

Phases of Bibliotherapy

Optimally as we read stories with students, we help them move through five phases: (a) involvement, (b) identification, (c) catharsis, (d) insight, and (e) universalism (see Table 2.1; Heath, Sheen, Leavy, Young, & Money, 2005). Initially, we invite students to listen to the story, to look at the pictures, and to become engaged in the story (*involvement phase*).

Table 2.1
Phases of Bibliotherapy

Phase	Description
Involvement	Students become interested as they look at the book's pictures and listen to the story
Identification	Students identify with story characters and situations
Catharsis	Students become emotionally engaged and vicariously experience the characters' feelings
Insight	Students relate the story to their own personal situation
Universalism	Students gain a broader perspective, helping them feel that they are not alone and that others struggle with similar challenges

In the *identification phase,* we help our students identify with and relate to the story's characters. This helps students build connections between the story and their personal lives. As students identify with story characters, they delve deeper and begin building emotional connections. These emotional connections help students feel what the characters are feeling (*catharsis phase*). During this phase, we need to carefully monitor students' emotional responses. Students need assurance that they are not alone and that caring adults are available to offer support. When students have extreme emotional reactions, we should consult with school-based mental health professionals.

By identifying and discussing both emotional and informational aspects of the story, we help students make sense of and understand the story's core message (*insight phase*). Then, with the story's leverage, we support students in building connections between the story and reality. In the *universalism phase*, students incorporate "lessons learned" into real-life daily activities. This phase helps students break from feelings of isolation, broadening their perspective to acknowledge that others struggle with similar challenges. It helps them understand that they are not alone.

The following example demonstrates how a teacher might implement the five phases of bibliotherapy in a classroom. This example stems from a common problem: a student being excluded and teased.

During recess duty one day in mid-September, first-grade teacher Miss Miller notices Devaun standing by the wall while the other students play games. The following week, Miss Miller notices the same pattern. Concerned about Devaun's limited social interaction with classmates, Miss Miller watches the other students more intently during recess and throughout each day. She notices a small group of students in her class deliberately and repeatedly excluding Devaun and ridiculing the way she dresses. One student in particular appears to be the ringleader, instigating the bullying. Miss Miller speaks directly with this student about the bullying. She then lets Devaun know that she is aware of what is happening and that she will help her feel more included by her peers. Miss Miller also speaks with the kindergarten teachers and gathers more information about whether bullying occurred last year. She also speaks with the school psychologist, who recommends that Miss Miller use bibliotherapy to support the schoolwide anti-bullying program.

After consulting with the school librarian, the school psychologist suggests several children's books and Miss Miller reads them, selecting a few that align most closely with her classroom's situation. Miss Miller sends a note home with all her students, sharing information with the parents about the upcoming unit on bullying. She asks for their support in discussing pro-social skills with their children, particularly focusing on helping everyone feel included.

Miss Miller then gathers her students together and introduces the first book. The book includes examples of relational and verbal bullying and has colorful pictures, an engaging story line, and is easy to share in a large group. She shows the cover of the book and asks the students a couple of questions to pique their interest (involvement). Holding the book for all to see, she reads the book with emotion, character voices, and enthusiasm. The book has several characters and situations with which students can relate (identification).

After reading the book to her students, Miss Miller pairs the students to discuss basic questions about the characters and situations in the story. Then students share their insights with the whole class, strengthening emotional connections with the story's characters (catharsis). Following the discussion, Miss Miller has the students complete an activity that compares and contrasts the story's situations with situations they have personally experienced or witnessed (insight). Concluding the bibliotherapy lesson, Miss Miller summarizes the book's core message and makes connections with students' experiences and situations in the school and community (universalism).

She then watches more closely at recess and during the school day to ensure that lessons taught through bibliotherapy are being practiced. During the school year, she continues to share books with her class that reinforce concepts taught about preventing bullying—taking a stand against bullying, stepping in when bullying is observed, and speaking up for oneself and others.

Rationale for Implementing Bibliotherapy in Schools

Expanding beyond the clinical setting, Forgan (2002) recommended teachers and parents use bibliotherapy with children to teach social skills and to address normal developmental challenges. Further endorsing bibliotherapy's use in nonclinical settings, Prater, Johnstun, Dyches, and Johnstun (2006) recommended teachers use bibliotherapy in classrooms to address the needs of vulnerable students. Heath et al. (2005) suggested that school personnel, such as school psychologists, school counselors, and social workers, use bibliotherapy when working with students who struggle with challenging emotions and behaviors. Additionally, bibliotherapy may be utilized when a student's Individual Education Program (IEP) specifies weekly counseling to address aggressive and bullying behavior. In addressing these needs, school-based mental health professionals may elect to use specific children's books aligned with counseling goals.

From a practical perspective, faced with tight school budgets, bibliotherapy is a cost-effective intervention. Additionally, educators have easy access to a wide range of children's books in school and public libraries. Staying in close touch with anti-bullying efforts, librarians can purchase books that best fit students' needs, selecting books that emphasize pro-social support and inclusive classroom environments. Likewise, teachers and school-based mental health professionals can consult with librarians about the specific bullying situations their students are facing and prescriptively match children's needs with specific books. As books are purchased, librarians can keep school personnel abreast of the library's newest additions.

Additionally, bibliotherapy is school and student friendly. Children love stories. In particular, classroom activities and related discussions extend selected stories into children's daily lives. Selected stories can clarify major teaching points, such as helping students understand that bystanders outnumber bullies. As such, bystanders hold the greatest power. Bystanders can speak up and confront bullies, who are in the minority. Understanding this shift in power will help students and educators more effectively counter and extinguish bullying behaviors.

Reading selected stories with students provides a fun group experience. This experience strengthens group cohesiveness, a critical element of building bystander support. Reading with a group of children becomes a shared experience that offers opportunities to teach social skills and to expand children's understanding of others' viewpoints (Hillsberg & Spak, 2006). Classroom bibliotherapy reduces isolation, helping children feel a part of the group (Forgan, 2002).

Selecting Books for Bibliotherapy

To address bullying, experts in the area of bully prevention recommend sharing stories with children (Berger, 2007; Teglasi et al., 2007). Olweus, considered to be the father of bullying research, stated: "The goal in reading aloud from the literature should be to increase the students' empathy with victims of bullying and to demonstrate some of the mechanisms involved, without teaching new ways of bullying" (1993, p. 82).

As educators, we must carefully select children's books, identifying books that promote supportive peer relationships, the benefits of friendship, and positive relationships between students and educators. Selected stories should model desired behaviors that counter bullying, such as sensitivity to others' feelings, kindness, cooperation, and taking appropriate action to support classmates. We must clearly define our expectations for children's attitudes and behaviors, particularly emphasizing the importance of sensitively considering and responding to classmates' feelings. Then, considering these expectations, we strategically identify books that model desired pro-social behaviors (Henkin, 2005). In sharing carefully selected books, we help classrooms build social support and strengthen students' resilience against bullying's negative impact (Davidson & Demaray, 2007).

In agreement with Olweus's goal, suggested books for bibliotherapy are included in Chapters 3 and 4. Additional resources are included in Appendix A. Acknowledging differences in classroom dynamics and the unique nature of situations that arise during the school year, we must carefully review books and resources to ensure a good fit with our students' needs. In addition to fun and entertaining stories and activities, core messages must support school and classroom rules. More specifically, stories and activities must model desired bullying resolution strategies and portray appropriate responses of adults, victims, and bystanders.

Because hundreds of children's books have been written on the topic of bullying, when selecting a book, we benefit from our librarian's expertise and familiarity with available bully-themed books. We must carefully consider how a specific book portrays bullying, how children and adults respond to bullying, and how bullying situations are resolved. Unfortunately, many stories promote bullying resolution strategies that clash with school rules and desired behavior. For example, books may include retaliation, physically fighting the bully, or embarrassing the bully. Henkin (2005) also warned about selecting unrealistic bully-themed books (e.g., the bully and victim immediately become best friends; the victim uses magical powers to change the bully). Optimally, stories' bullying situations should be resolved in both a pro-social and realistic manner.

The following guidelines are recommended for selecting bully-themed books for classroom bibliotherapy:

- Clearly identify desired bully resolution strategies that align with school and classroom rules, and then select books that model these strategies.

- Discuss book options with children's librarians and school-based mental health professionals, taking into account students' special needs, levels of maturity (cognitive, physical, social, and emotional), attention spans, interests, and individual characteristics (e.g., gender, cultural and ethnic background, socioeconomic status, and religious beliefs).

- Select books with clear and easy-to-understand core messages that focus on positive behaviors (what students should do) rather than on negative behaviors (what they should *not* do).

- Pre-read selected books to ensure appropriate content (e.g., language and illustrations) and to ensure core messages are both age appropriate and fully aligned with school/classroom rules and character values. Reading books in advance increases awareness of the story line and prepares educators to address subtleties that otherwise might be missed.

When selecting books, educators must consider students' unique needs and the types of bullying situations our students face. These considerations will increase the likelihood of children relating to the story's bullying situation. The stronger the association with the story, the more likely children will be to change their ways of thinking and behaving to align with the story's example (Gregory & Vessey, 2004).

To assist us in identifying books for bibliotherapy, a few authors have summarized information about bully-themed books. Oliver, Young, and LaSalle (1994) analyzed resolutions to bullying situations in 22 bully-themed fictional books written for intermediate and middle school students. Their analysis indicated that a third of the books (7 out of 22) featured main characters who sought revenge by physically fighting with the bully. After the fight, victims expressed rejuvenation and pride. Additionally, physical fighting with bullies was portrayed as effective in stopping bullying. However, because fighting runs counter to school rules, this strategy should not be promoted in schools. Only 3 of the 22 books portrayed bullies as ultimately coming to an understanding that bullying was wrong. Coping strategies were identified as either short-term or long-term. One of the most common short-term strategies was avoiding the bully. However, this strategy was portrayed as ineffective in stopping the bully's attacks.

Similarly, Entenmen, Murnen, and Hendricks (2005) analyzed 25 bully-themed children's picture books published between 1995 and 2003. Their analysis indicated the most frequently portrayed type of bullying was teasing and name calling (verbal intimidation); boys were more frequently portrayed as bullies than were girls; and the locations where bullying occurred were most frequently school and home. Included in 88 percent of the books (22 of the 25 books), bystanders most commonly helped victims. When adult characters were included in stories, they typically supported victims and taught victims how to cope with bullying. The most common strategy employed by victims was to stand up to the bully. Tension between the bully and victim was most commonly resolved by helping or making the bully learn how it feels to be victimized.

Extending Entenmen et al.'s study, Moulton, Heath, Prater, and Dyches (2011) analyzed 38 bully-themed children's picture books published between 2004 and 2010. All selected books were reviewed and ranked by *The Horne Book Guide* and received a rating of 1 to 4 (1 is the highest rating). Books that received a rating of 5 or 6 (considered poor ratings) were not included. Based on content analysis of the 38 selected books, males were more commonly portrayed as bullies (74 percent of the books portrayed male bullies); females were more commonly portrayed as victims (68 percent); and animal characters—rather than human characters—were included in almost half of the books. Of the books with human characters, the majority of bullies and victims were Caucasian.

Moulton et al. (2011) also described characteristics of victims. These descriptors included being short (most common characteristic of portrayed victims), tall, thin, heavy, shy, and overly sensitive. Other traits included dressing differently, lacking social power, and being a recent move-in. Verbal bullying was most frequently represented (79 percent, 30 of 38 books). Over half of the books included physical bullying (63 percent, 24 of 38 books). Relational bullying (e.g., excluding, ostracizing, gossiping) was included in seven books (18 percent).

In Moulton et al.'s (2011) analysis, the majority of bullying occurred in schools and neighborhoods. Bystanders, included in 25 of the 38 books (66 percent), responded to bullying by sticking up for victims, indirectly supporting victims (befriending and consoling), ignoring bullies, not intervening to stop bullying, laughing or smiling (supporting bullies), joining in with bullies, and telling an adult authority.

Detailed analyses, such as in Moulton et al.'s study, identify specific ingredients in bully-themed books and help us narrow options when selecting books for bibliotherapy. Each of the bully-themed picture books included in Chapters 3 and 4 is described in detail, including descriptions of characters (bully, victim, and bystander), bullying situation, and how the bullying is resolved. These important descriptors help us better understand the nature of bullying portrayed in the story.

Guidelines for Sharing Stories with Students

When introducing the selected book, we begin by asking a few questions. This creates interest and helps children focus their attention. These initial questions help students think about the book's message and may initiate discussion about children's experiences with bullying. An easy and natural way to introduce the book is to display the book's cover and, if available, briefly describe background information on the author and illustrator.

When we read stories aloud, students bond with each other and with the teacher in this shared activity. Additionally, all students are able to take part, regardless of their reading level. Children's interest increases when stories are read with feeling and enthusiasm. When we match our expression to realistically reflect characters and situations, stories are brought to life and students naturally identify with characters' feelings. Another suggestion to help maintain students' interest is to select books with large pictures that are easily shared, visible, and appealing to children (Sipe, 2008).

After reading the story, ask questions that encourage student discussion. By involving students in discussion of the story's major tenets, we are able to address misunderstandings and clarify points of confusion. In addition to post-reading discussion, learning should be solidified with an applied activity that enhances and personalizes the story's core message. Examples of activities include drawing pictures, participating in role-plays, playing games, and performing puppet shows.

In order to link the story's message to daily activities, we need to remind students of the story's core message. Referring to the story's relevant examples helps students strengthen targeted social skills and adaptive coping strategies. One example is to refer to "catch phrases" from stories. This helps create a common language for students and educators and becomes a fun shortcut for cuing students about appropriate and expected attitudes and behaviors. For instance, prior to excusing class for recess, teachers might say, "No *Mean Jeans* on our playground" (referring to Mean Jean, *The Recess Queen*). Or, when addressing students' teasing and name calling, we might offer the reminder, "It's what's in the can that counts" (referring to the post-reading activity associated with the book *I Like Who I Am*).

Offering additional insights, a list based on Prater el al.'s (2006) suggestions for successfully implementing bibliotherapy in classrooms is included in Table 2.2. To more fully understand bullying, it is important to monitor and describe bullying behavior across settings, gathering feedback from educators, staff, parents, and students. Additionally, the importance of collaborating with parents cannot be overemphasized. It is important to keep parents informed about a classroom's goals to strengthen bystander support. Help parents understand that we are encouraging children to take a stand against bullying, to step in, and to speak up. Brief home notes describing the books being read in the classroom will keep parents in the loop. Parents are then able to help their children generalize desired attitudes and behaviors that are being taught at school.

Table 2.2
A Guide for Using Bibliotherapy in the Classroom[a]

Suggested Strategies	Examples
Build strong relationships with students	Be honest, fair, and reliable when interacting with students. Let them know you are someone they can turn to when needed.
Collaborate with school professionals who can assist with bully prevention efforts	Identify a colleague you would like to work with in bully prevention efforts (e.g., teacher, librarian, counselor, school psychologist, social worker, parent volunteer) and solicit his or her commitment to help.
Invite parents' input and support	Invite parents to participate by sending a newsletter explaining the identified goals, describing selected books, and requesting their opinions regarding the selected books.
Define specific bullying problems students are experiencing	To more clearly identify bullying problems, observe student behavior across school settings and gather information from educators, school staff, administrators, parents, and students.
Set classroom goals to decrease bullying and identify strategies to achieve those goals	*Goal:* Increase the number of times bystanders speak up when they see bullying. *Strategy:* Use bibliotherapy to teach this skill. Role-play scenarios students might face and model expectations for bystander support.
Consult with librarian to select bully-themed books that fit students' needs	Ask librarian to identify books that address bullying and bystander support for victims, considering details specific to your students (e.g., age/grade, specific interests, unique situations).
Share several selected bully-themed books with students, observing their initial response	Allow students to express their interest or disinterest. Which books do they prefer?
Include reading activities that increase understanding and encourage discussion	Encourage children to use clues (e.g., pictures, details in story) to make predictions about what will happen next; read the section that either confirms or fails to confirm their predictions; change predictions to fit what actually occurs in the story; redefine predictions (Directed Reading and Thinking Activity; Reading Rockets, n.d.). Compare and contrast the story's details with students' lives.
Involve students in post-reading activities that stretch the story's core messages into real-life application	Include writing and art activities related to the story, such as journaling and drawing pictures. For example, ask students to write a letter to one of the story's characters or to make a collage of pictures representing story characters' feelings.
Monitor bibliotherapy's impact on students	Closely observe students' behavior. Ask questions such as: Are student bystanders taking a stand against bullying, stepping in, and speaking up for victims? Have bullying incidents decreased?

[a] This information was adapted from Prater et al. (2006).

After implementing bibliotherapy, it is important to take the additional step of monitoring our intervention's impact on students' behavior (Prater et al., 2006). Most importantly, we must be watchful of student behavior, determining if student bystanders are taking a stand against bullying, stepping in, and speaking up for victims.

Organizing Bibliotherapy with Lesson Plans

To assist us in implementing bibliotherapy and to help organize the essential elements and activities of bibliotherapy, this book includes structured lesson plans. Dovetailing on traditional lesson plans, lesson plans included in Chapters 3 and 4 contain the following elements: (a) an overall lesson objective related to bullying, (b) materials needed for implementing the lesson plan, (c) questions to be used as a basis for discussion before and after reading the book, and (d) additional activities to enhance the story's core message into real-life application. These basic elements are listed and described in Table 2.3.

Understanding the importance of tailoring lesson plans and activities to each specific group of children, Appendix A contains an annotated bibliography of additional resources, including a supplementary list of children's bully-themed books and books recommended to help children better understand emotions and feelings. The appendix also contains informational books for educators and Internet links to helpful handouts describing bullying and additional ideas for student learning activities.

Table 2.3
Basic Outline of Bibliotherapy Lesson Plan

Lesson Plan	*Description of Activities*
Pre-reading questions and discussion	Ask questions to stimulate student interest. This helps children focus their attention on the topic and builds anticipation and curiosity. This also creates a context for the story and helps educators assess students' initial knowledge and assumptions. In addition to asking questions, pre-reading also includes teaching key vocabulary.
Reading the book	Read aloud with enthusiasm, displaying the pictures for all students to see.
Post-reading activity and discussion	Children participate in activities and discussion that extend the story's core message into real-world application. Activities may include role-plays, games, individual worksheets, and creative activities aligned with the story's core message. Discussion further clarifies the story's core message and provides opportunities to check for students' understanding.
Closure	Educator clarifies and reemphasizes the major points and take-away message. In regard to attitudes and behaviors, educator clearly identifies what is expected of students and describes how to apply the story's lesson in day-to-day activities.

Chapter 3

LESSON PLANS TO STRENGTHEN BYSTANDER SUPPORT

The right story at the right moment is an arrow to the heart. It can find and catch what is hiding inside the reader (or the listener), the secret hurt or anger or need that lies waiting, aching to be brought to the surface.

—B. Coville, 1990, p. 35

This chapter contains lesson plans based on 15 selected bully-themed picture books, each designed to strengthen bystanders, encouraging them to take a stand, step in, and speak up against bullying. The silent majority of bystanders need encouragement and support, strengthening them to take a visible and vocal stance against bullying. Speaking up against bullying demonstrates personal responsibility for maintaining civility in our classrooms and for protecting others from bullying. This is an important and empowering life skill.

In working with students, we understand that children are particularly vulnerable to name calling and teasing. In comparison to physical bullying, verbal bullying is equally or more devastating to students. Additionally, when students are excluded (relational aggression), they suffer emotional pain, which fuels anger and resentment, increasing the potential for explosive acts of violence.

Reading children's bully-themed books helps students feel included and helps them discover the power within themselves and the collective power of classmates standing together against bullying. The lesson plans included in this chapter will fortify classrooms, creating a safe refuge against bullying and exclusion. In later years students will remember these stories and the kindness of educators and peers who took a stand, stepped in, and spoke up against bullying. Students will remember our efforts in making classrooms safe and inclusive.

As a quick overview of the 15 lesson plans included in this chapter, Table 3.1 succinctly summarizes each book's core message. Each lesson plan provides basic information, including the book's title, author, illustrator (if different from the author), publisher, year of publication, ISBN identifiers, number of pages and reading level (by grade and month), and estimated interest level. A brief synopsis of the story highlights the plot and resolution to bullying situations. Additional information describes supplementary resources included in the book. Descriptions of characters and bullying situations are listed in a table preceding each lesson plan. These descriptions include the type of character (e.g., animal or human); gender, age, and race of bully and victim; age difference between bully and victim; type of bullying; location of bullying; victim's response to bullying; bully's response to bullying; bystander's response to bullying; and resolution of bullying. This information gives a quick synopsis of important details to consider when selecting a book to share with children.

Each lesson plan format includes the following ingredients: (a) descriptive information (book title, author and illustrator, year of publication, and publisher); (b) reading level and interest level; (c) lesson objectives; (d) materials needed to teach lesson; (e) pre-reading activities (questions to stimulate interest and discussion); (f) key vocabulary; (g) sharing the story; (h) post-reading discussion; (i) extension activities; and (j) closure. By following the outlines, educators are able to present lesson plans with minimal preparation.

Table 3.1
Chapter 3: Books and Core Messages

Book	Core Message
The Bully Blockers Club	Strategies to stop bullying may work in some situations, but not in others. Bystanders must band together and support each other.
Chrysanthemum	Teasing and making fun of others is unkind. Students must speak up when a classmate is being teased.
Feathers	Gossip spreads unkind words. Don't repeat unkind words: "Don't pass it on: Gossip hurts."
Howard B. Wigglebottom Learns about Bullies	When bullied, we should follow our intuition and tell an adult. Remember, "Be brave, be bold, a teacher must be told."
I Get So Hungry	Speak up and support those who are teased for being overweight.
I Like Who I Am	When teased about our appearance (what we look like on the outside), remember that our true identity is inside our heart.
The Juice Box Bully	We stick up for each other when we see bullying.
Leave Me Alone	If one person is afraid to confront a bully, bystanders can band together and protect the victim.
Lucy and the Bully	Victims are not alone. When bullied they can tell trusted friends, teachers, and parents.
Nobody Knew What to Do	When students witness bullying, don't stand by and watch—tell a trusted adult, such as a teacher.
The Recess Queen	We do not want "bully power" ruling our playground. Playground rules help all students enjoy recess without fear of being bullied.
Say Something	Never remain silent when witnessing bullying. Befriend victims.
Stand Tall, Molly Lou Melon	Believe in yourself. Your weaknesses can become your strengths.
Yoon and the Jade Bracelet	True friends do not take advantage of each other. Bystanders and adults can support victims by stepping in and speaking up.
Don't Laugh at Me	Our individual characteristics make us unique. We should not be teased, left out, or ridiculed because of these traits.

The Bully Blockers Club

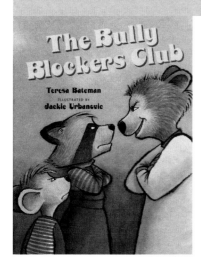

Author: Teresa Bateman
Illustrator: Jackie Urbanovic
Publisher: Albert Whitman
Year: 2004
ISBN: 0-8075-0919-1
ISBN 13: 978-0-8075-0919-7
Number of Pages: 32 (not paginated)
Reading Level: 2.9 (grade level)
Interest Level: PK+

Synopsis: Although Lotty is excited to start a new school year, it gets off to a rocky start when she is bullied by another student, Grant. Lotty is afraid to tell her teacher or others at school but confides in her brother and sister. They give her ideas—which she tries, but the strategies don't work. When Lotty watches Grant bully other students, she decides to form a student club to watch out for one another. At the same time, her teacher talks to the class about the difference between bullying and being friends. In the end, Grant no longer bullies and even helps Lotty.

Additional Information: The author provides an acronym, **TELL IT**, to help students remember the steps in reacting to bullying. **TELL IT** stands for **T**hink before you react; **E**xpress yourself—clearly state how you feel; **L**eave the situation—walk away; **L**augh it off—use humor to defuse the situation; **I**gnore the bully; and **T**ell a trusted adult.

Key Characteristics of Book's Characters and Bullying Situation	
Type of Characters	Animals
Bully's Gender, Age, & Race	Male, elementary age
Victim's Gender, Age, & Race	Female, elementary age
Bully's Age Compared to Victim	Same
Type of Bullying	Physical (taking things, kicking back of chair), Verbal (name calling)
Location of Bullying	Classroom, playground, lunchroom
Victim's Response to Bullying	Ignoring, being nice, making it a joke, standing up to bully
Bully's Response to Bullying	Additional name calling; after being confronted about bullying, he turns red (embarrassed) and returns items
Bystander's Response to Bullying	Laughter, looking away, standing up for victim
Resolution	Students create club for peer support; teacher talks about bullying

Lesson Plan 3.1
The Bully Blockers Club

Book: *The Bully Blockers Club* by Teresa Bateman, illustrated by Jackie Urbanovic (2004), Whitman & Co.

Reading Level: 2.9 (grade level)
Interest Level: PK+

Lesson Objective(s): Teach appropriate ways to stop bullying. After listening to the story, students will learn the TELL IT strategy and will role-play using the strategy.

Materials: Copy TELL IT (activity 3.1—part 1) for each student; 6 Popsicle/craft sticks for each student; crayons to color activity 3.1—part 1; glue; 1 premade set of TELL IT sticks; and scenarios (activity 3.1—part 2) on pages following *The Bully Blockers Club* lesson plan

Pre-Reading Activities	• Ask students if they get excited at the start of a new school year. What makes students nervous about starting a new school year? Has anyone started a new school year at a different school? • State, "Today we are going to read a story about Lotty, who is starting the first day of school but someone in her class is not nice to her. How do you think that will make her feel?" • Show the book's front cover (three characters) and ask who they think Lotty and her classmates are.
Key Vocabulary	**tattletale, karate chop, prickled, smack, allergic, grownups, clubs, bullying** • Review key vocabulary: Inform students, "In this story you may hear a few words that may be unfamiliar to you." Either write words on the chalkboard/whiteboard or type and use word strips. • Show each word (one at a time) and ask, "Who can tell me what this word means?" With student input, briefly define word and use the word in a sentence as an example.
Read the Story	
Post-Reading Discussion	*Review the book—show pictures and ask the following questions:* • Why do you think Lotty tells her brother and sister about Grant's bullying but not other people? • Lotty's brother suggests fighting Grant. Why is this not a good idea? • What are the other students doing in the pictures? Why do you think some laugh and others look scared or look away? What should they do? What would you do? • Do you think this club will work? Why or why not? What type of students could make this club work? • What made Grant stop bullying? Why?
Extension Activities	• Retell the story emphasizing what did and did not stop Grant's bullying. Emphasize that even though Lotty tried ignoring him and tried to be his friend, those ideas didn't work. Sometimes these ideas might work, but these ideas did not work with Grant. • Teach students the TELL IT system. Discuss which of these steps worked for Lotty (think before you react, tell others) and which didn't seem to help (leave the situation, laugh it off, ignore the bully). Ask students what else Lotty might do to stop the bullying (she didn't try expressing herself).

(continued)

Lesson Plan 3.1
(Continued)

Extension Activities	• Provide students the TELL IT Activity 3.1—part 1. Have students color each strategy as indicated with the specific strategy (e.g., Think before you react—yellow). Have them cut out each, fold them in half (on dotted line), place a Popsicle/craft stick in the middle, and glue together. Before starting the activity, be certain to make one set of TELL IT sticks for the teacher. • Have one student (without looking) draw one of the teacher's sticks. Select a few students to act like bullies. Role play the scenarios provided—activity 3.1—part 2 (or create your own) with the educator acting as the victim and responding according to the chosen stick (e.g., ignoring the bully, expressing yourself). • Have the other students guess which one is being role-played and hold up their corresponding stick. Because the different strategies are colored, the teacher can scan the classroom to see if they got it correct. • After modeling all of the strategies, place students in groups of three or four and have them role-play the same situations, switching roles from being the bully and the victim. • Bring the whole class together again. Have one student draw one of the teacher's sticks without looking. Then select one of the groups to role play the situation in front of the class. Have the other students guess which strategy is being role-played and hold up their corresponding stick.
Closure	• Review the TELL IT system. • Remind students that you will be watching for them to use these strategies with other students.

Think before reacting. (yellow)

Express yourself. (green)

Leave the situation. (red)

Laugh it off. (orange)

Ignore the bully. (purple)

Tell a trusted adult. (blue)

Activity 3.1—part 2 *The Bully Blockers Club*

Scenarios

(1) Susan is a new student in the class. She is short in size and wears glasses. Students in another class start calling her "Shorty" and "Four-Eyes" on the playground. They point to her and whisper to each other, calling her these names.

(2) Walter isn't very good at playing sports. During recess, students never invite him to join in their games. One day Walter tries to join in on a four-square game. He gets in line to join the game, but when it is his turn, George tells him he can't play. When Walter doesn't leave, George pushes him away from the game and tells him to never come back.

(3) Natasha doesn't read very well. When she reads out loud, the teacher has to help her with a lot of the words. Students don't laugh at her while in reading group, but when the teacher isn't looking they call her "stupid" and "dummy."

(4) Moki and Muna are twin brothers who just moved to a new school. They are the only Native Americans in the school. They are in the same classroom and stick together on the playground, on the bus, and in the lunchroom. The other students think the brothers' names are funny and begin calling them "Coke" and "Tuna."

(5) Lydia is overweight for her age. She lives down the street from one of her classmates, Jessica, but they have never really been friends. During one summer they start playing together, but at the end of summer before school starts, Jessica tells Lydia not to tell anyone that they are friends. Lydia ignores Jessica during the school day. When another student tells Jessica she saw her playing with Lydia on Saturday, Jessica says it's not true.

Book Summary 3.2
Chrysanthemum

Author: Kevin Henkes
Publisher: HarperCollins Publishers
Year: 1996 (reprinted)
ISBN: 0-688-14732-1
ISBN 13: 978-0-688-14732-7
Number of Pages: 32 (not paginated)
Reading Level: 3.3 (grade level)
Interest Level: PK+
Available in Spanish: *Crisantemo*

Synopsis: Chrysanthemum considered her name to be "absolutely perfect." However, classmates ridicule her unique and lengthy name. One classmate notes that Chrysanthemum's name is spelled with 13 letters—half of an alphabet! Chrysanthemum wishes for another name, something short, simple, and normal, like her classmates' names. The pregnant music teacher, Mrs. Twinkle, overhears the students' teasing and laughter. She informs the children that her lengthy name (Delphinium) is also a flower and that she is considering the name Chrysanthemum for her baby—because it is an "absolutely perfect" name. Subsequently, the teasing stops, classmates respect Chrysanthemum's name, and she regains appreciation for her name.

Additional Information: This book is also available in large paperback (18.9" × 15.3"; ISBN 978-0061119743). Larger pictures make it easier to share stories with children.

Key Characteristics of Book's Characters and Bullying Situation	
Type of Characters	Animals (mice)
Bully's Gender, Age, & Race	Primary bully is female, early elementary
Victim's Gender, Age, & Race	Female, early elementary
Bully's Age Compared to Victim	Same
Type of Bullying	Verbal
Location of Bullying	Classroom, playground
Victim's Response to Bullying	Embarrassment, sadness
Bully's Response to Bullying	Continues, enjoys taunting and put-downs, gains strength as a ringleader
Bystander's Response to Bullying	Others join in bullying, laughing
Resolution	Bullying stops when the music teacher asks questions, getting to the bottom of the teasing. She announces she might name her new baby Chrysanthemum.

From *Classroom Bullying Prevention, Pre-K–4th Grade: Children's Books, Lesson Plans, and Activities* by Melissa Allen Heath, Tina Taylor Dyches, and Mary Anne Prater. Santa Barbara, CA: Linworth. Copyright © 2013.

Lesson Plan 3.2
Chrysanthemum

Book: *Chrysanthemum* by Kevin Henkes (1996—reprinted), HarperCollins Publishers

Reading Level: 3.3 (grade level)
Interest Level: PK+

Lesson Objective(s): To teach children to take a stand, step in, and speak up when a classmate is teased. After listening to the story, students will participate in a role-play and create (as a group) a paper chrysanthemum with each student's name on a petal. The classroom flower will be posted on the bulletin board as a reminder of the book's message.

Materials: Yellow and orange construction paper for "flower petals" (see directions and pattern on *Chrysanthemum* activity sheet). Cut one flower petal for each class member and one for the teacher; glue; 28" × 22" poster board; crayons or markers; three phrases (cut from *Chrysanthemum* activity sheet and pasted on flower stem)

Pre-Reading Activities	*Show the outside cover of the book and ask the following questions:* • Who can say the word "chrysanthemum"? Let's all try to say this word. • What is a chrysanthemum? • Is anyone in our class named Chrysanthemum? • Do you know anyone whose name is Chrysanthemum? • Think about your name—How did you get your name? • Explain that this book is about a little mouse named Chrysanthemum. • Ask the students to think about how Chrysanthemum feels about her name and to listen to what classmates say about her name.
Key Vocabulary	**precious, priceless, fascinating, winsome, miserably, jealous, begrudging, discontented, jaundiced, indescribable, wilted, dreadful, humorous** • Review key vocabulary: Inform students, "In this story you may hear a few words that may be unfamiliar to you." Either write words on the chalkboard/whiteboard or type and use word strips. • Show each word (one at a time) and ask, "Who can tell me what this word means?" With student input, briefly define word and use the word in a sentence as an example.
Read the Story	
Post-Reading Discussion	*Review the book—show pictures and ask the following questions:* • How did Chrysanthemum get her name? • How do we know that Chrysanthemum likes her name? • Why did the other students giggle (laugh) when they heard Chrysanthemum's name? • How did Chrysanthemum's parents describe her name? • What is Mrs. Twinkle's first name? • After hearing that Mrs. Twinkle might name her baby Chrysanthemum, how did the students feel about Chrysanthemum's name? • When the story ended, how did Chrysanthemum feel about her name?

(continued)

Extension Activities	In this story, Victoria was the ringleader in teasing and saying unkind things about Chrysanthemum's name. Other students joined in with Victoria when they laughed and said unkind things. Sometimes one student takes the lead in teasing another student—this is the ringleader because he or she is the leader of the group causing trouble. When we see someone being unkind, how can we stop the teasing before it spreads? Should we wait for a teacher (like Mrs. Twinkle) to step in, take a stand, and speak up? Can kids step in, take a stand, and speak up to help stop teasing?
	
	ROLE-PLAY
	Introduce the role-play by reading page 15 that begins with "'She even looks like a flower,' said Victoria, as Chrysanthemum entered the playground. 'Let's pick her,' said Rita, pointing. 'Let's smell her,' said Jo."
	
	• Explain that sometimes students might say something unkind. However, others do *not* need to join in by adding more unkind words. Students make a choice as to whether they will or won't laugh and join in with teasing and saying unkind things.
	• Role-play the book's playground scene and identify different comments classmates might make to support Chrysanthemum.
	  ○ Rather than joining in with Victoria, identify what Rita and Jo could say to support Chrysanthemum. Suggest supportive comments that do *not* join in with Victoria. Explain: There is only one Victoria on the playground. A lot of other kids on the playground can take a stand, step in, and speak up. What could these kids say? Write students' ideas on the board.
	  ○ Assign parts for Victoria, Rita, Jo, Chrysanthemum, and several bystanders. NOTE: Except for Victoria, all the classmates should support Chrysanthemum.
	  ○ Write simple phrases for participants and make sure students understand their part in the role-play. The following script is an example.
	    Victoria: "She even *looks* like a flower."
	    Rita: "I think flowers are beautiful."
	    Jo: "Chrysanthemum is a beautiful name."
	    Other bystanders: "You can play with us, Chrysanthemum."
	
	ACTIVITY (activity 3.2)
	Pass out pre-cut flower petals (one for each student) and crayons or markers.
	Directions: Ask students to write their name on their flower petal.
	They may also color or draw pictures describing their name.
	When completed, paste each petal on the giant classroom chrysanthemum.
	Paste the phrases, "Take a stand; Step in; Speak up," on the flower's stem. Remind students to think about others' feelings. The classroom flower reminds students to speak up when they see bullying.

Closure	• **Write on the board**: "I can speak up." • **Explain**: This story was about Victoria and others teasing Chrysanthemum. When we see others teasing someone, we do *not* join in the teasing. Together, we can speak up and *stop* the teasing. Just as Mrs. Twinkle does, when teachers and staff see teasing, they will ask questions and talk with students to identify bullying. Our classroom chrysanthemum reminds us that all of us together are stronger than one bully.

Flower Petal Pattern

Directions: Make petals with bright yellow and orange construction paper. Cut one flower petal for each student. Ask students to write their name on their petal. They can also draw pictures or words that describe who they are. Paste petals in a circular pattern on a 28" × 22" poster board (resembling a chrysanthemum).
Draw a flower stem and glue the three phrases on the flower's stem.

Take a stand; Step in; Speak up

From *Classroom Bullying Prevention, Pre-K–4th Grade: Children's Books, Lesson Plans, and Activities* by Melissa Allen Heath, Tina Taylor Dyches, and Mary Anne Prater. Santa Barbara, CA: Linworth. Copyright © 2013.

Book Summary 3.3
Feathers

Author: Heather Forest
Illustrator: Marcia Cutchin
Publisher: August House Publishers
Year: 2005
ISBN: 0874837553
ISBN 13: 978-0874837551
Number of Pages: 32 (not paginated)
Reading Level: 2.8 (grade level)
Interest Level: K+

Synopsis: This story is based on an Eastern European folktale. A woman accused of starting rumors (gossip) is brought before the town's religious leader (rabbi). The rabbi listens as the gossiping woman makes excuses and avoids taking responsibility. She claims she intended no harm: she was merely joking. The gossiping woman apologizes and "takes back her words." Worried that the woman underestimates the harm caused by gossiping, the rabbi directs the woman to take a feather pillow to the market square, cut the pillow open, release the feathers, and then gather up every single feather. The woman discovers it is impossible to collect all the feathers. With remorse she acknowledges that, similar to her actions with the feathers, she cannot take back her gossip.

Key Characteristics of Book's Characters and Bullying Situation	
Type of Characters	Humans
Bully's Gender, Age, & Race	Female, adult, eastern European (Jewish)
Victim's Gender, Age, & Race	Female, adult, eastern European (Jewish)
Bully's Age Compared to Victim	Appears to be same age
Type of Bullying	Verbal (gossiping)
Location of Bullying	Community (village)
Victim's Response to Bullying	Crying, embarrassment
Bully's Response to Bullying	At first the bully minimized and denied the harm, claiming words were said in jest—then, with a forced apology, the bully assumed the problem was easily forgiven.
Bystander's Response to Bullying	Evidently bystanders participated in the bullying by spreading the gossip.
Resolution	Rabbi (religious leader) confronts woman's gossiping by teaching a lesson with a bag of feathers (difficult to take words back after they are released). The gossiping woman ultimately admits to the extensive damage caused by gossiping and the impossibility of retrieving unkind words once they are released.

From *Classroom Bullying Prevention, Pre-K–4th Grade: Children's Books, Lesson Plans, and Activities* by Melissa Allen Heath, Tina Taylor Dyches, and Mary Anne Prater. Santa Barbara, CA: Linworth. Copyright © 2013.

Lesson Plan 3.3
Feathers

Book: *Feathers* by Heather Forest, illustrated by Marcia Cutchin (2005), August House Publishers

Reading Level: 2.8 (grade level)
Interest Level: K+

Lesson Objective(s): To demonstrate the harm caused by unkind words (gossip). This story counters the often quoted "sticks and stones may break my bones, but words can never harm me." After listening to the story, students will participate in a class activity and then discuss the following points: Unkind words hurt. Gossip spreads unkind words. To prevent gossip, do not spread unkind words: "Don't pass it on, Gossip hurts."

Materials: Three feathers; crayons; feather activity 3.3; scissors (to cut feather bookmark); paper punch and string to hang feathers from the ceiling—or use the feathers as bookmarks.

Pre-Reading Activities	*Show the outside cover of the book and ask the following questions:* • This picture shows a kitten playing with something we do not usually see floating around in the air. What is this? [*point to feather on book cover*] • This word [*point to the book's title*], "Feathers," is the title of this book. • How would you describe a feather? [*Show students three feathers*] • Ask three students to come to the front of the room. Place one feather in the palm of each student's hand and give the following directions to the student volunteers: Blow the feathers. Describe what happened when you blew the feather. • Some people say, "Sticks and stones may break my bones, but words can never harm me." This statement is not true. When we use unkind words, it really hurts others. Listen to this story about a woman who gossiped and spread rumors.
Key Vocabulary	**gossip, rumor, rabbi, jest, justice, amends, crime, accused, careless, excused, humor, snatch, weary, scattered, cruel, rind** • Review key vocabulary: Inform students, "In this story you may hear a few words that may be unfamiliar to you." Either write words on the chalkboard/whiteboard or type and use word strips. • Show each word (one at a time) and ask, "Who can tell me what this word means?" With student input, briefly define word and use the word in a sentence as an example.
Read the Story	
Post-Reading Discussion	*Review the book—show pictures and ask the following questions:* • What is a rumor? [*give an example*] • Why would someone start a rumor? • Why would someone spread a rumor? • How do you stop a rumor? • This woman says, "What I said was in jest, just humor." This is like kids using the excuse, "I was just kidding!" She also blames others for spreading gossip. She is not taking responsibility for her behavior. • What is a rabbi? [*a teacher and religious leader in the Jewish community*]

(continued)

Post-Reading Discussion	• How far away are these feathers floating? Do you think you could gather up all these feathers? • When the woman returns to the rabbi, does she look different than when she first met with the rabbi? Explain the differences.
Extension Activities	**ACTIVITY** • Ask students to form a circle. • Explain the game "Pass It On." This game shows how quickly and easily a story changes as it passes from one person to another. This shows how gossip spreads. • Teacher starts the message. One at a time, each student quietly whispers to the person next to them until the message moves all the way around the circle and back to the teacher. • Each person can only whisper the message one time. If the listening person does not clearly hear the message, they must whisper the message to the next person, saying what they think they heard. • Whisper the following message to the first student: • "Suzette took some silly string from Sam's locker because she wanted some. She didn't get paid her allowance until Saturday." • After the message goes all the way around the circle, compare the end message with the initial message. • Emphasize the following point: Gossip and mean words hurt. "Don't pass it on: Gossip hurts." Gossip stops when mean comments and rumors are not passed on to others. **ACTIVITY** See activity 3.3. Make a copy for each student. Have students decorate, then cut out the feather bookmark with the phrase, "Don't pass it on: Gossip hurts." Either hang these feathers from the ceiling (use paper punch and tie a string to each feather) or use as a bookmark.
Closure	**Write on the board**: *Don't pass it on: Gossip hurts.* **Read the final page of the book**: "Cruel words like feathers fly. Cruel words reach far and wide. They leave the mouth a bitter rind. May all your words, my friends, be kind."

Activity 3.3   *Feathers*

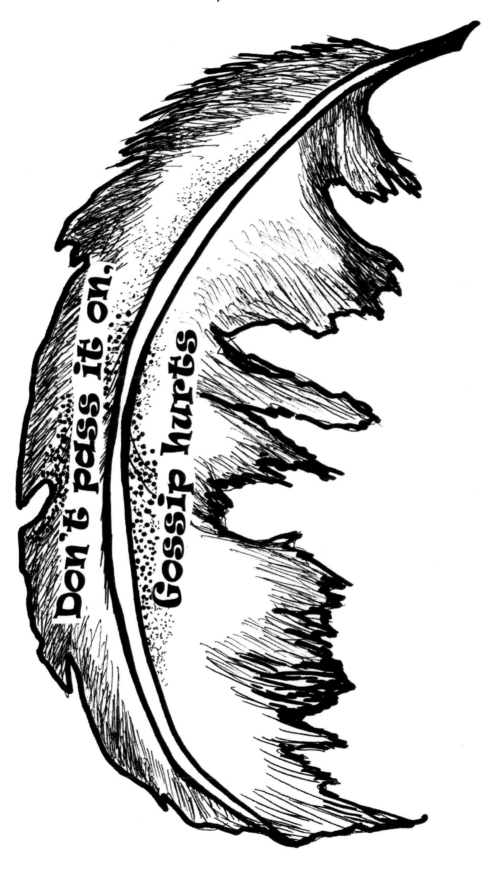

Don't pass it on.

Gossip hurts

Howard B. Wigglebottom Learns about Bullies

Author: Howard Binkow
Illustrator: Susan F. Cornelison
Publisher: Thunderbolt
Year: 2010 (second printing)
ISBN: 0-9715390-3-0
ISBN 13: 978-0-9715390-3-7
Number of Pages: 32 (not paginated)
Reading Level: 3.4 (grade level)
Interest Level: PK+

Synopsis: Howard B. Wigglebottom has a hard time sleeping because he knows the next day he will be bullied by the Snorton twins, who will push him down, take his lunch, and make him eat worms. His intuition tells him, "Be brave, be bold, a teacher must be told." After using his imagination to get away from the bullies fails, he tells his teacher, who tells the principal, who tells the twins' parents. Howard B. Wigglebottom then feels safe and is able to sleep at night.

Additional Information: Lessons and reflections are included at the back of the book. Additional resources, including an animated storybook, accompanying rap song, interactive discussion questions/answers, posters, and lessons are available at www.wedolisten.com.

Key Characteristics of Book's Characters and Bullying Situation	
Type of Characters	Animals
Bully's Gender, Age, & Race	Male and female, elementary age
Victim's Gender, Age, & Race	Male, elementary age
Bully's Age Compared to Victim	Same
Type of Bullying	Physical, verbal
Location of Bullying	Outside, in classroom
Victim's Response to Bullying	Fear, uses imagination to think of scenarios to get away from bullying, then tells his teacher
Bullies' Response to Bullying	Continue to bully, fight with each other, learn an important lesson
Bystander's Response to Bullying	Victim imagines bystanders calling him a "tattler"
Resolution	Bullies fight with each other, then learn an important lesson

From *Classroom Bullying Prevention, Pre-K–4th Grade: Children's Books, Lesson Plans, and Activities* by Melissa Allen Heath, Tina Taylor Dyches, and Mary Anne Prater. Santa Barbara, CA: Linworth. Copyright © 2013.

Lesson Plan 3.4
Howard B. Wigglebottom Learns about Bullies

Book: *Howard B. Wigglebottom Learns about Bullies* by Howard Binkow, illustrated by Susan F. Cornelison (2010), Thunderbolt

Reading Level: 3.4 (grade level)
Interest Level: PK+

Lesson Objective(s): To teach students to tell an adult when they are being bullied or when they see someone being bullied. Students will draw pictures to illustrate telling a teacher when they are bullied or see someone being bullied.

Materials: Audiofile of the "Be Brave, Be Bold" song; animated storybook; discussion questions—all available on the Internet website [www.wedolisten.com]; paper; crayons/markers; activity 3.4 (rap)

Pre-Reading Activities	• After discussing the front cover of the book with the students, tell them that you want them to repeat the phrase whenever they see it in the book, "Be brave. Be bold. A teacher must be told."
Key Vocabulary	**"little voice in his head," brave, bold, "fist-punching," "name-calling," "worm-whomping," "tongue-wagging," "foot-stomping," tattletale, snitch, cloak, invisible, twirl, hurl, outer space, stubby legged, amazement, drifted, imagination** • Review key vocabulary: Inform students, "In this story you may hear a few words that may be unfamiliar to you." Either write words on the chalkboard/whiteboard or type and use word strips. • Show each word (one at a time) and ask, "Who can tell me what this word means?" With student input, briefly define word and use the word in a sentence as an example.
Read the Story	
Post-Reading Discussion	*Review the book—show pictures and ask the following questions or have students answer these discussion questions on the website [www.wedolisten.com]. For interactive discussion questions, click on "Lessons and Poster," then "Howard B. Wigglebottom Learns about Bullies."* • Why was Howard afraid to go to school? • What did the Snorton twins do that made Howard sad? • Did the Snorton twins bully in front of their teacher? • When the Snorton twins were fighting, was Howard a bully, a bystander, or a victim? • Why did it take so long for Howard to tell the teacher? • What did the little voice in Howard's head keep telling him? • Who did Howard finally tell? • Who can you talk to if you or someone else is being bullied?
Extension Activities	• View the animated book on the website [www.wedolisten.com]. • Refer to activity 3.4. Have students draw pictures to illustrate the "Be Brave, Be Bold" rap, then use the pictures to perform the rap in front of the class.
Closure	Ask students what Howard B. Wigglebottom finally did to stop the bullying (told his teacher). Remind students that pretending to be invisible or to have superpowers is not likely to stop bullying. Repeat the phrase, "Be brave. Be bold. A teacher must be told."

"Be Brave, Be Bold" Rap

Transcribed song from http://wedolisten.org/media/songs.html

You gotta be brave
B.R.A.V.E., that's what you gotta be
Say it's a part of me
(*repeat*)

Got to be brave, got to be bold
Do the right thing—let a teacher be told
Do the right thing—yes, this is so
Mr. Wigglebottom—now he knows
(*repeat*)

You gotta be brave
B.R.A.V.E., that's what you gotta be
Say it's a part of me
(*repeat*)

You gotta be brave

What should I do? What should I say?
Should I say anything or should I pay?
A little voice in my head saying it's ok
Go ahead and tell your teacher—you can be brave

The next day I waited after class,
When everybody left, then the teacher asked
What's the matter, son, why you look so sad?
I said the bully in the back has been treating me bad
I said all the bad things the bully did

Then the bully finally stopped
When I told the teacher all the things he did
Then the teacher called his pop

You gotta be brave
B.R.A.V.E., that's what you gotta be
Say it's a part of me
(*repeat*)

You gotta be brave

You can do it—you're brave
Yes, you really are
Don't be afraid to say what's in your heart
(repeat)

Got to be brave, got to be bold
Do the right thing—let a teacher be told
Do the right thing—yes, this is so
Mr. Wigglebottom—now he knows
(*repeat*)

You gotta be brave
B.R.A.V.E., that's what you gotta be
Say it's a part of me.
(*repeat three times*)

You gotta be brave

From *Classroom Bullying Prevention, Pre-K–4th Grade: Children's Books, Lesson Plans, and Activities*
by Melissa Allen Heath, Tina Taylor Dyches, and Mary Anne Prater. Santa Barbara, CA: Linworth. Copyright © 2013.

I Get So Hungry

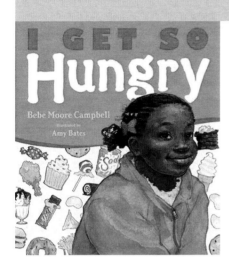

Author: Bebe Moore Campbell
Illustrator: Amy Bates
Publisher: Putnam Juvenile
Year: 2008
ISBN: 0399243119
ISBN 13: 978-0-399-24311-0
Number of Pages: 32 (not paginated)
Reading Level: 2.9 (grade level)
Interest Level: 1+

Synopsis: Teased for being overweight, Nikki follows the example of her teacher and decides to live a healthier lifestyle. She begins walking with her teacher before school and walking with her mother on the weekends. She also starts eating healthier foods. Her friends stand up for her when the bully teases her for being overweight and calls her names.

Key Characteristics of Book's Characters and Bullying Situation	
Type of Characters	Humans
Bully's Gender, Age, & Race	Male, elementary age, African American
Victim's Gender, Age, & Race	Female, elementary age, African American
Bully's Age Compared to Victim	Same
Type of Bullying	Verbal (name calling)
Location of Bullying	Classroom
Victim's Response to Bullying	Feels sad, eats more food, pretends that she is eating the bully
Bully's Response to Bullying	Continues to call names, eventually laughs when bystanders defend the victim
Bystander's Response to Bullying	Friends tell the bully that it's "not funny," to "be quiet," and call him a name
Resolution	Victim begins a healthier lifestyle; bystanders verbally confront the bully

Lesson Plan 3.5
I Get So Hungry

Book: *I Get So Hungry* by Bebe Moore Campbell, illustrated by Amy Bates (2008), Putnam Juvenile

Reading Level: 2.9 (grade level)
Interest Level: I+

Lesson Objective(s): To teach students to demonstrate respect for self and others by using kind words and by developing healthy eating and exercise habits. Students will identify activities that demonstrate kindness to others and activities that match a healthy lifestyle.

Materials: From magazines, cut pictures of junk foods (e.g., French fries, cookies, soda, ice cream, doughnuts, cupcakes, fried chicken, candy, chips). Based on negative words from the story, write a negative word on the back of each picture (e.g., "supersize," "fatty"); "Healthy Kids" BINGO cards (*I Get So Hungry* activity pages); healthy snacks for final party

Pre-Reading Activities	Tape pictures of junk foods on the board. Ask students to pick one food that they like from the board. Then have them turn the picture over and read the word that is listed. Ask them how they would feel if someone called them that word, or words that mean the same thing. Tell the students you are going to read a story about a girl who is teased for being overweight.
Key Vocabulary	**gobble, checkups, deserve, diet, thinner, fried food** • Review key vocabulary: Inform students, "In this story you may hear a few words that may be unfamiliar to you." Either write words on the chalkboard/whiteboard or type and use word strips. • Show each word (one at a time) and ask, "Who can tell me what this word means?" With student input, briefly define word and use the word in a sentence as an example.
Read the Story	
Post-Reading Discussion	*Review the book—show pictures and ask the following questions:* • What do you notice about Mrs. Patterson? (Emphasize that she appears to be compassionate, creative, and funny.) • How do Sarah and Keisha react to Arnold's name calling? • Why do you think Nikki eats when she feels sad? • Why do you think it is hard for Nikki to stop eating once she starts? • Why do you think Mrs. Patterson turned around and coughed when she wanted to eat the cookie? • Why does Nikki pretend that each chip she eats is Arnold Inksley? • What does Nikki do well? (*sing*) Do you think Arnold realizes this? Why/why not? • Why do you think it's hard for Nikki and her mom to stop eating "junk food"? • What does Mrs. Patterson do to get healthy? (*eat healthy food, exercise, eat junk food only once in a while*) • How do Nikki's friends defend her when Arnold yells, "Nikki Thicky"? Rather than calling Arnold a name, what might be another way to defend Nikki?

(continued)

Lesson Plan 3.5
(Continued)

Extension Activities	Have students create their own "Healthy Kids" BINGO cards by drawing pictures or writing words in each BINGO cell of activities related to exercising/increasing physical activity, eating healthy foods, and being kind to others. Encourage students to identify realistic and obtainable goals. Post students' BINGO cards on the classroom wall. After completing a listed activity, students will "X" over the activity. Encourage students to support each other in completing all of their activities within a set time period (e.g., two weeks). Once all students have reached "Blackout" (all spaces are crossed out), have a healthy snack party and a fun group activity. Third- and fourth-grade students will write down 24 activities. Younger students (first- and second-grade students) will write down 14 activities. Pre-K and K students will all use one of the two "Healthy Kids" BINGO cards with pictures (see Pre-K and K "Healthy Kids" BINGO cards).
Closure	Healthy kids are those who are kind to each other and make healthy eating and activity choices. You have learned how to make good decisions that help others and that lead to a healthy lifestyle.

HEALTHY KIDS BINGO
Pre-K and K

Images retrieved from Microsoft Clipart

HEALTHY KIDS BINGO
Pre-K and K

B	I	N	G	O
		FREE		

Images retrieved from Microsoft Clipart

From *Classroom Bullying Prevention, Pre-K–4th Grade: Children's Books, Lesson Plans, and Activities*
by Melissa Allen Heath, Tina Taylor Dyches, and Mary Anne Prater. Santa Barbara, CA: Linworth. Copyright © 2013.

HEALTHY KIDS BINGO

Suggested Activities for Grades 1–4

Ride my bike
Eat vegetables at dinner
Play basketball

Go on a walk with my mom/dad
Drink milk, not soda
Walk to school
Play dodge-ball at recess
Eat a healthy snack after school
Try rollerblading or skating
Help a younger child
Help weed the garden
Do 50 sit-ups
Play catch with my brother/sister
Ask a lonely kid to play at recess
Push a child in a wheelchair to the lunchroom

Make a tossed salad for dinner
Run around the playground
Play four-square
Blow bubbles outside
Do 20 pushups
Vacuum the living room
Eat a new vegetable for dinner
Water the flowers/garden
Drink three glasses of water in one day
Eat three fruits today
Do 20 gentle stretches

Take my dog for a walk
Eat no more than one candy today
Play tag with friends
Use kind words with kids who are different from me

Clean my room rather than watch TV
Do 100 jumping jacks
Walk with my friends before dinner
Jump rope for 10 minutes
Run in place during TV commercials
Dance to my favorite song
Swim for 15 minutes
Eat carrots for a snack
Try a new fruit
Play softball
Jump on a trampoline
Play basketball
Play tennis
Play soccer
Sweep the porch/sidewalk
Say something kind to a classmate
Try to see both sides of an argument
Speak kindly to kids on school bus
Play tag at recess
Eat popcorn for a snack
Write a "thank-you" note
Eat an orange

From *Classroom Bullying Prevention, Pre-K–4th Grade: Children's Books, Lesson Plans, and Activities* by Melissa Allen Heath, Tina Taylor Dyches, and Mary Anne Prater. Santa Barbara, CA: Linworth. Copyright © 2013.

HEALTHY KIDS BINGO
Grades 1–2

B	I	N	G	O
		FREE		

HEALTHY KIDS BINGO
Grades 3–4

B	I	N	G	O
		FREE		

I Like Who I Am

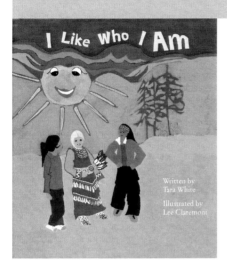

Author: Tara White
Illustrator: Lee Claremont
Publisher: Theytus Books
Year: 2010
ISBN: 1894778634
ISBN 13: 978-1894778633
Number of Pages: 40
Reading Level: 3.5 (grade level)
Interest Level: 2+

Synopsis: Celina and her mother recently moved to a community of Native Americans. Although Celina is a Mohawk, she looks different than other Native American children. She has blonde hair and blue eyes. One classmate, Becky, repeatedly confronts Celina about these visible differences and says, "You are not a Mohawk." Becky and her friends band together against Celina. However, Heather befriends Celina. Becky's continual badgering discourages Celina. Celina begins to question her identity. In a private discussion, her great-grandma teaches Celina that who you are is not based on outward appearances and others' perceptions of you. Who you are is how you live and what you think and believe. "It's about what's in your heart."

Key Characteristics of Book's Characters and Bullying Situation	
Type of Characters	Humans
Bully's Gender, Age, & Race	Female, elementary age, Native American
Victim's Gender, Age, & Race	Female, elementary age, Native American (Mohawk)
Bully's Age Compared to Victim	Attend the same classroom, but bully is taller
Type of Bullying	Physical (makes mean faces to intimidate victim), relational (excludes victim from group), verbal (identifies differences in appearance)
Location of Bullying	School playground and community pow wow
Victim's Response to Bullying	Sadness, withdrawal, questioning her identity
Bully's Response to Bullying	Increasing anger toward victim
Bystander's Response to Bullying	Bully's friends laugh at victim; one student befriends and includes victim in play, stands by victim, and reassures victim
Resolution	After victim shows dancing talent, bullying toward victim stops; then tables turn and bully becomes vulnerable; victim befriends bully and they become friends

Lesson Plan 3.6
I Like Who I Am

Book: *I Like Who I Am* by Tara White, illustrated by Lee Claremont (2010), Theytus Books

Reading Level: 3.5 (grade level)
Interest Level: 2+

Lesson Objective(s): To teach children it's what's inside that counts. Following the story, students will participate in the "Label and Can" activity. Students will describe things about themselves (personal appearances) that are readily apparent to others (the label). Then, in contrast, students will identify things about themselves that others might not notice, such as talents, personality traits, and beliefs (ingredients that are inside the can).

Materials: Copy of "Label" and "Can" worksheets for each student (Activity: *I Like Who I Am*); pencils or crayons; scissors (to cut label from worksheet); glue (to paste the label onto the can); can opener; one can of soup with a switched label—replace label on the can so the can's content and label do not match

Pre-Reading Activities	*Show the outside cover of the book and ask the following questions:* • This picture shows three girls who are in this story. Which one of these girls is not like the others? • What are the differences? • This story is about children who are Native American. What does Native American mean? • One tribe (group) of Native Americans is called Mohawk. Celina is Mohawk.
Key Vocabulary	**Mohawk, ignore, creation, blush, clenched, pow wow, culture, gaping, taunted, demonstration** • Review key vocabulary: Inform students, "In this story you may hear a few words that may be unfamiliar to you." Either write words on the chalkboard/whiteboard or type and use word strips. • Show each word (one at a time) and ask, "Who can tell me what this word means?" With student input, briefly define word and use the word in a sentence as an example.
Read the Story	
Post-Reading Discussion	*Review the book—show pictures and ask the following questions:* • (pages 10–11) Why would Becky blush? How do you feel when you do not know an answer to the teacher's question? • (page 12) What word describes how Becky might be feeling when she clenches her fists? [*demonstrate as you say the word "clenches"*] • (page 14) What is a "pow wow?" • (page 28) When Becky ran off, what do you think she was feeling? • (page 30) Why would Celina want to help Becky? • (page 32) Why would Celina yell, "I am Mohawk!" • Who helped Celina feel welcome in the new school? [*the classroom teacher and Heather*] • Did Becky help Celina feel welcome in the new school? • What did Becky keep saying to Celina? [*What are you doing here? You are not Mohawk. You have blonde hair and blue eyes.*]

(continued)

Lesson Plan 3.6
(Continued)

Post-Reading Discussion	• What reasons did Celina have for feeling she was Mohawk? [*She knows the Mohawk language; her name is Mohawk and means "the Creation is complete"; her relatives are Mohawk; and she knows the Native American dances. But most important of all, her great-grandma told her that she was Mohawk in her heart, in her thoughts, and in her actions.*] • (page 24) Near the end of the story, children who watched Celina dance stared with their mouths gaping open. What does this mean? [*demonstrate*] Why would the children be surprised about Celina's dancing?
Extension Activities	Show students the can of soup (with the switched label). Ask the following questions: • How do you know what type of soup is in this can? • What soup do you think is in this can? [*Allow students to guess, then open the can.*] • What kind of soup is actually in this can? Explain that the label on this soup led us to believe that a certain kind of soup was in this can. Sometimes we judge others by what is on the outside—what we see—rather than what is on the inside—who they really are. • Pass out the "Can" and "Label" activity sheets—one "Can" and one "Label" for each student, pencils or crayons, glue, and scissors. Pre-K–2nd grade will use the "Label" handout identified for that age group. Younger students will draw pictures and older children will write words to describe what others see on the surface (label). Third- and fourth-grade students will use the "Label" handout identified for that age group. All students use the "Can" worksheet. Inside the can, children will list (writing or drawing) their unique talents, skills, and interests. Offer examples to assist students in understanding what is expected of them. • After students have completed the "Can and Label" activity, ask students to share the differences between their label and the contents in their can.
Closure	*Draw a heart on the board.* **Explain**: The bigger part of who you are is deep inside you. As the great-grandma said, "It's about the way you live your life" and "what's in your heart." Don't tease someone because he or she looks different [*referring back to the "Can and Label" activity*]—it's what's inside the can that really counts.

Can (all ages)

Inside the can, write (or draw) your talents and interests that are important to you.

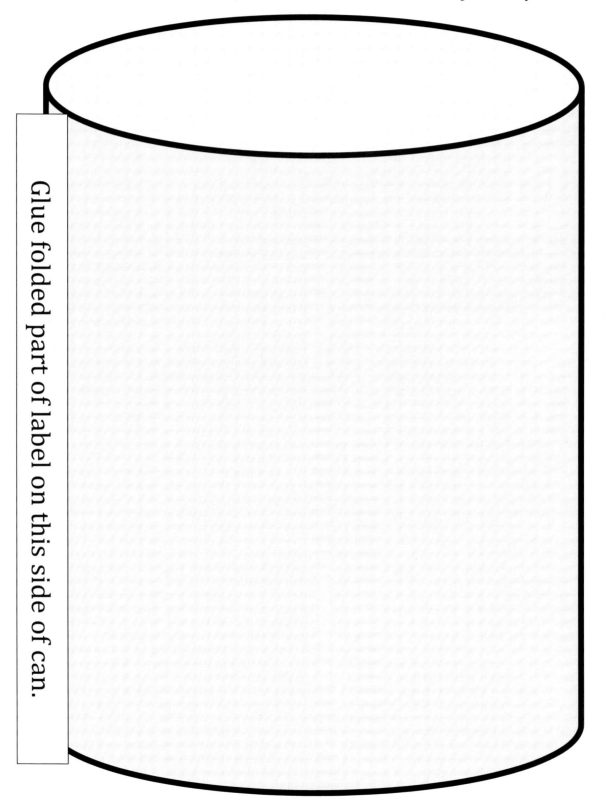

Glue folded part of label on this side of can.

Label (Grades PK–2)

Draw your face on this label. This label goes on the outside of your can. When others look at you, this is what they see (the color of your hair and eyes, your smile, the color of your skin). Cut out your label and paste one side on the can. After the glue dries, look at the label, and then pull back the label to see what is inside the can.

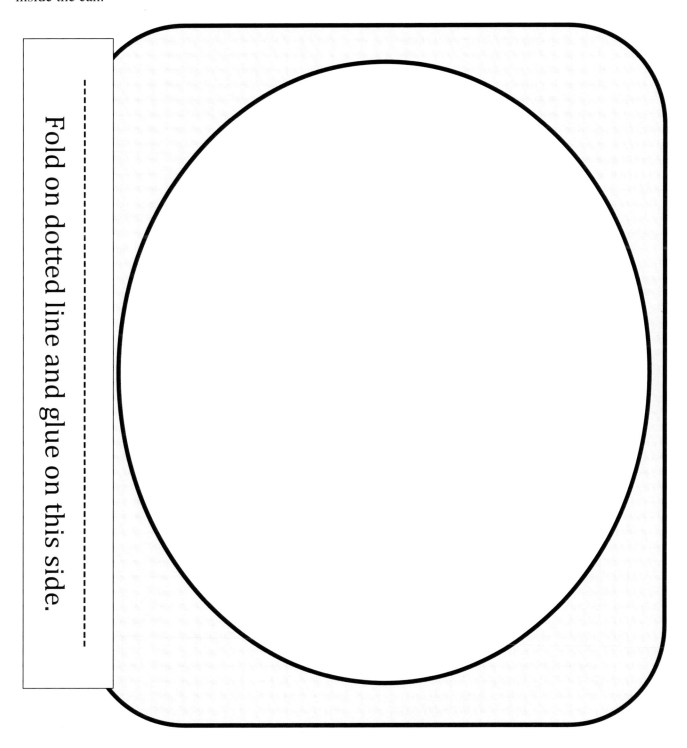

Fold on dotted line and glue on this side.

Label (Grades 3+)

This is a label. When others look at you, this is what they see. They do not see inside the can. Write a list of things others see when they first meet you. Cut out your label and paste the folded side of the label onto your can. After the glue dries, look at the label (what others see), and then pull back the label to see what is inside the can.

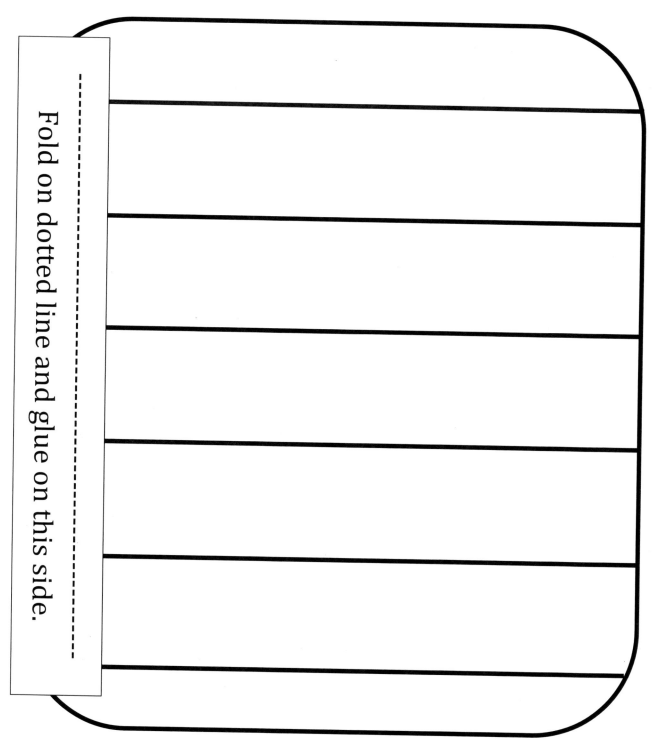

Fold on dotted line and glue on this side.

Book Summary 3.7
The Juice Box Bully

Author: Bob Sornson and Maria Dismondy
Illustrator: Kim Shaw
Publisher: Ferne Press
Year: 2010
ISBN: 1933916729
ISBN 13: 978-1933916729
Number of Pages: 32 (not paginated)
Reading Level: 3.0 (estimated)
Interest Level: 2+ (grade level)

Synopsis: Pete, a new student, watches as others play soccer. When Ralph asks him to join the game, he says, "Not with those nerds." Pete urges Ralph to help him steal the ball, but Ralph refuses. So, Pete does it himself. Ruby tells Pete about the class promise to take care of one another and to not allow bad behavior. Later, when Ruby asks Pete to play soccer, he squirts his juice box onto her shirt. She gets angry and wants to retaliate, but Ralph reminds her that the class promise doesn't allow retaliation. Pete notices that Ralph stands up for him. Ruby later apologizes. These actions make Pete interested in the class promise.

Additional Information: At the end of the book, "The Promise" is listed with a brief explanation about the importance of adults empowering children to take action when they witness bullying.

Key Characteristics of Book's Characters and Bullying Situation	
Type of Characters	Humans
Bully's Gender, Age, & Race	Male, upper elementary or middle school, Caucasian
Victim's Gender, Age, & Race	Male and female, upper elementary or middle school, Caucasian, Asian
Bully's Age Compared to Victim	Same
Type of Bullying	Physical (stealing ball, squirting juice on victim), verbal, (name calling)
Location of Bullying	Playground
Victim's Response to Bullying	Telling him not to do it, wanting retaliation
Bully's Response to Bullying	Continues bullying, then stops based on other students' reactions
Bystander's Response to Bullying	Stand up to the bullying
Resolution	Bully becomes interested in learning about "The Promise"

From *Classroom Bullying Prevention, Pre-K–4th Grade: Children's Books, Lesson Plans, and Activities*
by Melissa Allen Heath, Tina Taylor Dyches, and Mary Anne Prater. Santa Barbara, CA: Linworth. Copyright © 2013.

Lesson Plan 3.7
The Juice Box Bully

Book: *The Juice Box Bully* by Bob Sornson and Maria Dismondy, illustrated by Kim Shaw (2010), Ferne Press

Reading Level: 3.0 (estimated)
Interest Level: 2+ (grade level)

Lesson Objective(s): To teach the importance of sticking up for others when bullying is observed. After listening to the story, students will commit to taking the promise and role-play examples of following and not following the promise.

Materials: Poster board to list details of "The Promise"; pencils, crayons, or magic markers; copies of personal commitment to uphold the promise (activity 3.7—part 1); role-play scenarios (activity 3.7—part 2)

Pre-Reading Activities	Ask students to state their favorite juice flavor. Ask them how they would feel if someone splashed juice on their shirt on purpose. Explain that this story tells about someone who did this.
Key Vocabulary	**snarled, growled, spitefully, shrieked, demanded, bystander** • Review key vocabulary: Inform students, "In this story you may hear a few words that may be unfamiliar to you." Either write words on the chalkboard/whiteboard or type and use word strips. • Show each word (one at a time) and ask, "Who can tell me what this word means?" With student input, briefly define word and use the word in a sentence as an example.
Read the Story	
Post-Reading Discussion	*Review the book—show pictures and ask the following questions:* • Why do you think Pete pulls his hat down over his head when his teacher introduces him to his new class? • Why does Pete "growl" at Ralph? • Why do you think Pete doesn't want to join the game? • Why doesn't Ralph join Pete in stealing the ball? • What do you think the promise is? • Why do you think Pete squirts juice on Ruby's shirt? • How would you feel if you were Ruby? • Was Ruby right in feeling like she wanted to do something bad to Pete? Why/why not? • Why does Ralph stick up for Pete? • What does Pete tell Ralph about his old school? • Why does Pete change his mind about the promise?
Extension Activities	• With student assistance, make and post "The Promise" poster on a bulletin board. "The Promise" is found at the end of the book right before the author's and illustrator's biographical information page. Talk through each behavior listed. Role-play using the scenarios (activity 3.7—part 2). Ask students to act out the example of the promise and the example of not following the promise. This will help students differentiate between the two. • Using the splash handout (activity 3.7—part 1), ask students to commit to "The Promise." Have students sign the statement, then color the "splash" in their favorite juice color. Have students cut out the splash and post their pledges around "The Promise" poster.

(continued)

Lesson Plan 3.7
(Continued)

Closure	• Remind students that just like the students in the book, we are agreeing to use "The Promise" to help stop bullying in the school. Posting this on the bulletin board can help us remember our promise. • Throughout the year have students recite "The Promise" and discuss how this promise has worked or how the class could do better.

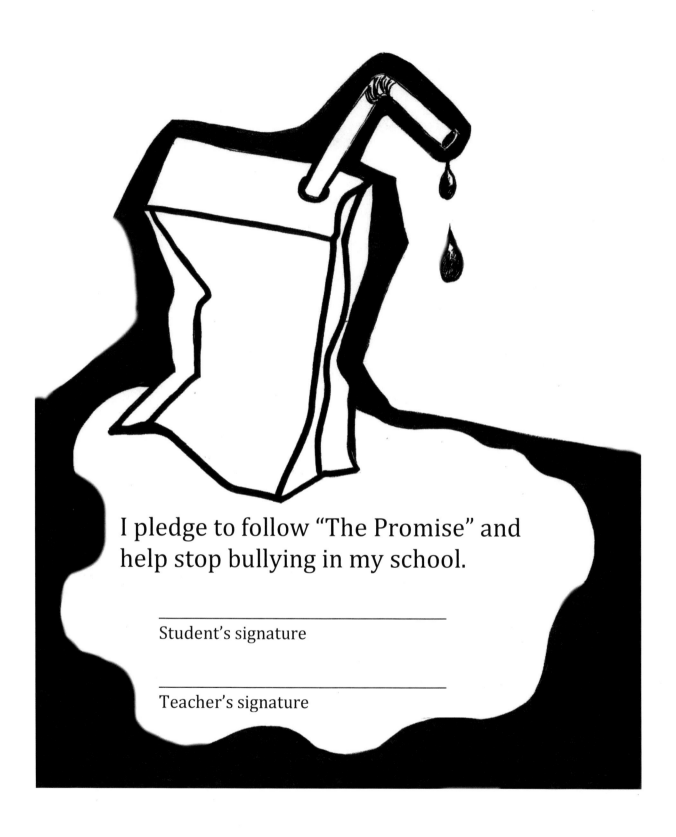

I pledge to follow "The Promise" and help stop bullying in my school.

_____
Student's signature

_____
Teacher's signature

Scenarios

Using the following brief scenarios, have students act out what keeping the promise would look like and what it would not look like.

What will I do?

1. I see Jonny hit Talita on the arm on the playground.

2. A new student, Harry, joins our class in the middle of the year. He is in a wheelchair and talks kind of funny.

3. Joseph hasn't been asked by anyone to play in the baseball game. I see him sitting on the side watching and he looks sad.

4. Penny tells me that she doesn't like my dress and that I look ugly. She suggests I go home and change before making the rest of the class sick with my looks.

5. I hear Farad tell Erica that if she doesn't give him her lunch money he will beat her up after school.

6. Rich asks me to join him in playing tricks on Vance. He wants me to put notes in Vance's lunchbox that call him names.

7. Reading is not easy for me. Every time the teacher asks me to read out loud several students laugh, not loud enough for the teacher to hear, but I can see their hands over their mouths and their shoulders going up and down like they are laughing.

8. When Billy gets off the school bus, he trips and falls. Several students stand around pointing at him, laughing, and calling him a "retard."

9. Yvonne and Averi have told me they don't want to play with me anymore. They ignore me and tell others not to play with me either.

10. I see George grabbing Owen's baseball cap off his head several times. He runs away with it eventually, leaving it somewhere on the playground where Owen has to look for it.

11. Nico is selected for the city's All-Star softball team. Demitri is angry that he was not selected. To embarrass Nico, Demitri starts a bad rumor about Nico's older sister.

Leave Me Alone: A Tale of What Happens When You Stand Up to a Bully

Author: Kes Gray
Illustrator: Lee Wildish
Publisher: Barron's Educational Series
Year: 2011
ISBN: 0-7641-4736-6
ISBN 13: 978-0764147364
Number of Pages: 32 (not paginated)
Reading Level: 1 (grade level)
Interest Level: PK+

Synopsis: "Leave me alone," says a young boy to many animals he encounters in a field. He rejects the help of these concerned friends, stating that his problem is too big for them. He reveals that his problem is that he is bullied daily by a giant "so big that he blocks the sun," casting a dark and long shadow over him. When the bully approaches, the animal friends stand up for the boy and yell, "Leave him alone!" Shocked, the confused bully sneers and walks away.

Key Characteristics of Book's Characters and Bullying Situation	
Type of Characters	Human, giant, and animals
Bully's Gender, Age, & Race	Giant
Victim's Gender, Age, & Race	Male, early elementary, Caucasian
Bully's Age Compared to Victim	Not clearly depicted
Type of Bullying	Verbal (intimidation)
Location of Bullying	Outside
Victim's Response to Bullying	Fearful, allows friends to stand up for him, feels confident the bully won't return
Bully's Response to Bullying	Bullies every day for fun; when confronted, bully is surprised and walks away
Bystander's Response to Bullying	Numerous friends take a stand and speak up, telling bully to "Leave him alone!"
Resolution	Bully walks away

From *Classroom Bullying Prevention, Pre-K–4th Grade: Children's Books, Lesson Plans, and Activities* by Melissa Allen Heath, Tina Taylor Dyches, and Mary Anne Prater. Santa Barbara, CA: Linworth. Copyright © 2013.

Lesson Plan 3.8
Leave Me Alone

Book: *Leave Me Alone: A Tale of What Happens When You Stand Up to a Bully* by Kes Gray, illustrated by Lee Wildish (2011), Barron's Educational Series

Reading Level: 1 (grade level)
Interest Level: PK+

Lesson Objective(s): To recognize when a friend needs someone to step in and stand up to a bully. After reading the story, students will act out how to come together as a group to stand up to a bully.

Materials: Source of light (flashlight, projector); white sheet hung in a darkened room; paper cut-outs representing each character in the story (or real objects); scissors; Popsicle/craft sticks; masking tape

Pre-Reading Activities	*Show the outside cover of the book and ask the following questions:* • Have you ever wanted to be alone? Why? • How do you feel when you're alone? • Look at this boy who is alone. How do you think he is feeling? • When we read this book, I want you to look on each page for shadows.
Key Vocabulary	**miserable, "pass you by," downhearted, sobbing, whiskers, wilt, chat, habit, giant, casts, firm, enemy, sneered, snarled, stomped** • Review key vocabulary: Inform students, "In this story you may hear a few words that may be unfamiliar to you." Either write words on the chalkboard/whiteboard or type and use word strips. • Show each word (one at a time) and ask, "Who can tell me what this word means?" With student input, briefly define word and use the word in a sentence as an example.
Read the Story	
Post-Reading Discussion	*Review the book—show pictures and ask the following questions:* • Show the first page of the bully's shadow and ask, "What do you think this is?" • Why do you think these animals want to help the boy? • Show the picture of the giant with red eyes. Ask, "How do you think the boy feels when this giant bullies him?" • Do the animals look scared of the giant? Why/why not? • How do you think the giant felt when the animals told him to leave their friend alone?

Extension Activities	**Shadow Play**
	
	• Assist students in reenacting the story with a Shadow Play.
	    ○ Using either hand shapes, real objects, or paper puppets taped on popsicle/craft sticks representing each character in the book, have students act out the story. Character silhouettes are on the *Leave Me Alone* activity pages.
	    ○ To project the objects' shadows, place the silhouettes between the light source and the sheet (hung from the ceiling). The audience should sit on the other side of the sheet where they can see the shadows cast on the sheet.

(continued)

Lesson Plan 3.8
(Continued)

Extension Activities	○ Move the characters of the book closer and then farther away from the light. How powerful (large) are they when they are close to the light? How does the shape/size of the shadows change with distance from the light? How powerful is the group when they are close together? How powerful are they when they are close to the bully? ○ Move all of the animal characters together so they are larger than the shadow of the bully. Discuss how sticking together brings power and confidence.
Closure	When you see a friend being teased or bullied, get together with some other friends and stick up for the victim. Together say, "Leave him/her alone!" You can help those who feel sad and powerless when you stand up to the bully.

Activity 3.8 *Leave Me Alone*

Lucy and the Bully

Author: Claire Alexander
Publisher: Albert Whitman & Company
Year: 2008
ISBN: 0-8075-4786-7
ISBN 13: 978-0-8075-4786-1
Number of Pages: 32 (not paginated)
Reading Level: 2.5 (grade level)
Interest Level: PK+

Synopsis: Classmates often ask Lucy to draw pictures for them. Tommy, jealous of Lucy's talent, spills paint across her painting, stomps her clay bird, and threatens Lucy not to tell on him. The bullying continues across time. Lucy does not want to tell her mother or teacher about the bullying. Against Lucy's pleadings *not* to call her teacher, Lucy's mother calls and reports the bullying. The teacher calls the bully's mother. To Lucy's surprise, the next day the bullying stops. Lucy notices a change in Tommy. He appears sad and withdrawn. During art class, Lucy compliments Tommy's drawing. Lucy asks Tommy to draw a picture for her. Tommy, both pleased and surprised, apologizes for his bullying. Lucy forgives him and they go outside to play.

Key Characteristics of Book's Characters and Bullying Situation	
Type of Characters	Animals
Bully's Gender, Age, & Race	Male, early elementary, animal (bull)
Victim's Gender, Age, & Race	Female, early elementary, animal (lamb)
Bully's Age Compared to Victim	Attend the same classroom, but bully is bigger
Type of Bullying	Physical (damages victim's artwork and materials), verbal (threatens her not to tell about bullying)
Location of Bullying	Classroom; outside school building after school
Victim's Response to Bullying	Fear, sadness, difficulty sleeping
Bully's Response to Bullying	Unbeknownst to teacher and classmates, bully continues damaging victim's things
Bystander's Response to Bullying	Unaware of bullying, bystanders are not present in pictures of bullying situations
Resolution	Victim tells mother; victim's parent and teacher intervene; teacher calls bully's mother; bullying stops; and victim and bully become friends.

From *Classroom Bullying Prevention, Pre-K–4th Grade: Children's Books, Lesson Plans, and Activities* by Melissa Allen Heath, Tina Taylor Dyches, and Mary Anne Prater. Santa Barbara, CA: Linworth. Copyright © 2013.

Lesson Plan 3.9
Lucy and the Bully

Book: *Lucy and the Bully* by Claire Alexander (author and illustrator), (2008), Albert Whitman & Company

Reading Level: 2.5 (grade level)
Interest Level: PK+

Lesson Objective(s): To teach that when students are bullied they can tell trusted friends, teachers, and parents. Students will identify individuals they can talk to about bullying. Students will participate in three role-plays to demonstrate what they will say to a friend, a teacher, and a parent.

Materials: Copy of "STOP" activity worksheet for each student; pencils or crayons; role-plays and name tags (activity: "Stop Bullying: Tell Someone"); scissors; masking tape

Pre-Reading Activities	*Show the outside cover of the book and ask the following questions:* • This picture shows two characters who are included in our story. Which one of these characters do you think is Lucy? • Lucy is "artistic." She draws and paints really great pictures. What types of thoughts and feelings might other students have when they see Lucy's beautiful pictures?
Key Vocabulary	**accident, model, jealous, artistic, crumpled, wailed** • Review key vocabulary: Inform students, "In this story you may hear a few words that may be unfamiliar to you." Either write words on the chalkboard/whiteboard or type and use word strips. • Show each word (one at a time) and ask, "Who can tell me what this word means?" With student input, briefly define word and use the word in a sentence as an example.
Read the Story	
Post-Reading Discussion	*Review the book—show pictures and ask the following questions:* • Everyone is coming to look at Lucy's painting. [*Read the students' comments about Lucy's painting, then point to Tommy.*] What do you think this student is feeling? • Why did Lucy's blackbird receive a gold star? • When someone stomps on something, what do you think they are feeling? • Why did Lucy not want to tell her mother about Tommy? • When Lucy could not sleep, what was she afraid of? • After the teacher and Tommy's mother talked with Tommy, why did he feel sad and alone? • When Lucy wanted Tommy to draw a hedgehog for her, why was Tommy surprised? • If you were Lucy, would you forgive Tommy?
Extension Activities	**Stop Activity** • Copy and pass out the "STOP" activity 3.9—part 1 with pencils or crayons to each student. • Explain: If you or someone you know is bullied, tell your friend, teacher, and parent. On the stop sign, write the names of three people you will tell. Write one name on each line. After you write the names, we will role-play to practice what we might say.

(continued)

Lesson Plan 3.9
(Continued)

Extension Activities	**Role-Plays** • Assign roles and act out the three scenarios from activity 3.9—part 2, role plays. • Cut out the name tags and tape the name tag on the student actor/actress.
Closure	**Write on the board**: *"Tell someone"* **Explain**: Today we read a story about Lucy and Tommy. When we are bullied, we need to tell our friends, our teacher, and our parents. We do not keep quiet about bullying. We are not alone. We can tell our friends. We can tell our teacher. We can tell our parents. They will help us speak out against bullying. We can all work together to stop bullying.

From *Classroom Bullying Prevention, Pre-K–4th Grade: Children's Books, Lesson Plans, and Activities* by Melissa Allen Heath, Tina Taylor Dyches, and Mary Anne Prater. Santa Barbara, CA: Linworth. Copyright © 2013.

I can tell my FRIEND, my TEACHER, and my PARENT

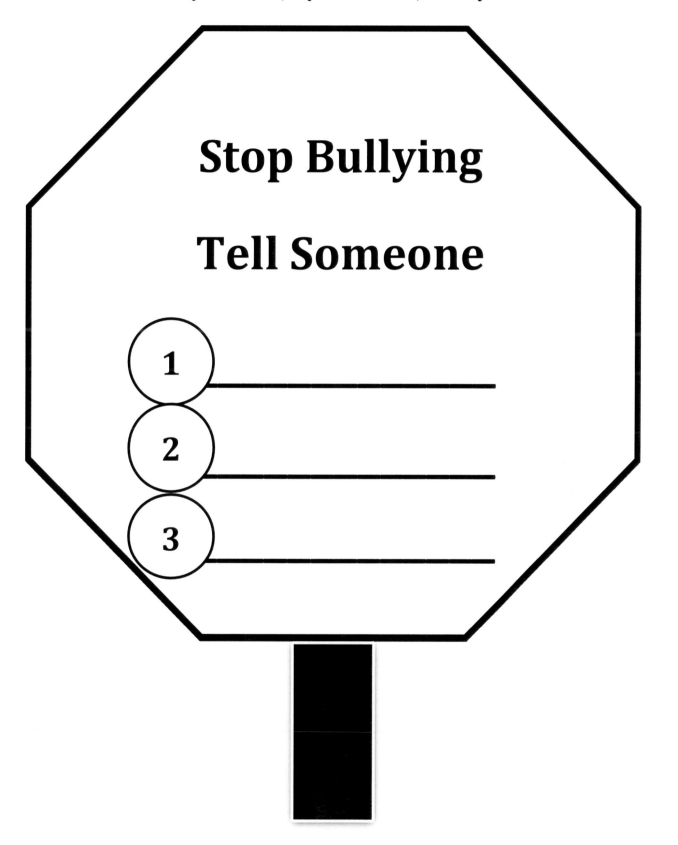

Stop Bullying

Tell Someone

1 _____

2 _____

3 _____

Role-Plays
Stop Bullying: Tell Someone

Role-Play #1: Tell a friend

Every day on the school bus two older boys trip Suzi, grab her backpack, and go through it looking for treats and money. The bus driver does not seem to notice. The boys tell Suzi she will be "sorry" if she ever tells anyone. When Suzi comes to school, Tim, a good friend, notices she is sad.

Tim	Suzi, you look sad. What's wrong? Please tell me.
Suzi	Two big boys on the bus are just awful to me.
Tim	What do you mean?
Suzi	Every day they trip me and grab my backpack. Then they take stuff out of my backpack.
Tim	Wow, those guys are bullies. This is not your fault. We need to tell our teacher and she will help us.
Suzi	Thanks, Tim. I feel better already.
Tim	Now let's go and talk to our teacher.

Role-Play #2: Tell a teacher

José is new to Hilltop Elementary School. José is learning English and has some trouble understanding what other children are saying. He often nods approval and smiles during recess. Several boys are teaching José bad words that will get him in trouble if a teacher hears him saying these words. The boys also slap José on the back really hard and tell him that "this is what friends do." José is uncomfortable and does not know what to do. José starts to cry. The boys make fun of him, saying "Sissy! Boys don't cry." When the recess bell rings, José returns to the classroom. The teacher, Mrs. Moreno, notices something is wrong.

Mrs. Moreno	José, is something wrong? You seem very sad.
José	I do not like recess. I want to go home.
Mrs. Moreno	Tell me why you do not like recess.
José	The boys are mean to me. They hit me on the back.
Mrs. Moreno	It is against the rules to hit. Do you know the names of the boys who hit you?
José	I do not know the boys. The boys are not in our class. They are in the other class.
Mrs. Moreno	Two students in our class, John and Tom, are good friends. They will help keep the mean boys away from you. You can join in with John and Tom and they will be your new friends. I will also talk with the teacher in charge of the playground. We do not allow bullying on our playground. José, we will make sure you are not bullied on the playground. Thank you for talking with me. It takes courage to tell a teacher.

(continued)

Role-Play #3: Tell a parent

During recess, Latosha wins all the jump rope games. She can jump for a long time without messing up. She can jump super-fast and do really cool jump rope tricks. Several of her friends (Sara, Julie, and Tami) are jealous. They make fun of her and call her "JRF—jump rope freak." They start a girls' club and tell Latosha that she cannot join. They tell all the other girls that whoever talks to Latosha cannot be part of the girls' club. Latosha is feeling very lonely and very sad. She decides to tell her mom.

Latosha	Mom, I really need to talk to you.
Mom	Latosha, is something wrong?
Latosha	Yes, all the girls at school are being mean to me.
Mom	That makes me sad! What are these girls doing?
Latosha	Sara, Julie, and Tami make fun of me. They call me "JRF," Jump Rope Freak. They started a girls' club and won't let me join. They said that anyone who talks with me can't join. Now nobody will talk with me.
Mom	That is bullying! I will talk with your teacher about this. This has gone way too far.
Latosha	Mom, please don't.
Mom	Latosha, this is not a good situation. The sooner we stop this from going on, the better. Your teacher and I can help stop this bullying. I know that this kind of bullying is making other kids feel uncomfortable too. We will be helping more kids than just you.

Cut out name tags for role plays.

Suzi	**Tim**
Mrs. Moreno	**José**
Latosha	**Mom**

Nobody Knew What to Do: A Story about Bullying

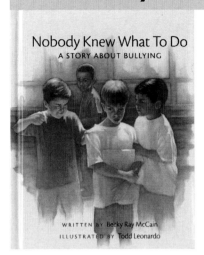

Author: Becky Ray McCain
Illustrator: Todd Leonardo
Publisher: Albert Whitman & Company
Year: 2001
ISBN: 0-8075-5711-0
ISBN 13: 978-0-8075-5711-2
Number of Pages: 32 (not paginated)
Reading Level: 2.7 (grade level)
Interest Level: PK+

Synopsis: Becoming increasingly upset from watching Ray being bullied, a classmate says he and others are uncomfortable but they don't know what to do about it. Too afraid to do anything, the bullying continues. When Ray does not come to school, the classmate overhears bullies planning to do bad things to Ray when he returns. The classmate tells the teacher about what he overheard. He also invites Ray to play with him. When the bullies attempt to bully Ray, the principal and teacher come to the playground and stop it. They call the parents of the bullies. The students now feel confident, knowing what to do when they see bullying.

Additional Information: Children have a hard time distinguishing between tattling and reporting an emergency or bullying situation. Tattling is spreading stories that don't need to be told with the intent of getting someone in trouble. Reporting is letting an adult know about an emergency or bullying situation. A note at the end of the book provides more information about bullying and tips for helping children through bullying situations.

Key Characteristics of Book's Characters and Bullying Situation	
Type of Characters	Humans
Bully's Gender, Age, & Race	Males, elementary age, mixed races
Victim's Gender, Age, & Race	Male, elementary age, Caucasian
Bully's Age Compared to Victim	Same
Type of Bullying	Physical (pushing, pulling, hitting, pinching, grabbing, stealing); verbal (yelling, name calling, threatening)
Location of Bullying	Classroom, playground, front of school
Victim's Response to Bullying	Stopped coming to school
Bully's Response to Bullying	Cheered
Bystander's Response to Bullying	Ignored, then told the teacher, and invited victim to play
Resolution	Teacher and principal intervened, called parents of bullies

From *Classroom Bullying Prevention, Pre-K–4th Grade: Children's Books, Lesson Plans, and Activities* by Melissa Allen Heath, Tina Taylor Dyches, and Mary Anne Prater. Santa Barbara, CA: Linworth. Copyright © 2013.

Lesson Plan 3.10
Nobody Knew What to Do

Book: *Nobody Knew What to Do: A Story about Bullying* by Becky Ray McCain, illustrated by Todd Leonardo (2001), Albert Whitman & Co.

Reading Level: 2.7 (grade level)
Interest Level: PK+

Lesson Objective(s): Teach children to combat bullying by gathering with friends and reporting to adults. Children will describe the difference between tattling and reporting.

Materials: Computer with Internet access; materials to make elephant trunks—gray paint, paintbrushes, empty cardboard paper towel rolls (one for each student), scissors, yarn

Pre-Reading Activities	• Play audio file of Camille Saint-Saens's "Elephant" from "The Carnival of the Animals" (http://www.teachertube.com/viewVideo.php?video_id=194264&title=The_Elephant_Double_Bass). • Ask the children to think which animal Saint-Saens is depicting in this clip. After describing an elephant, ask why they think it sounds like an elephant. Play a video file that incorporates both the music and video of elephants (http://www.youtube.com/watch?v=ug8hCAyBaqg; http://www.youtube.com/watch?v=kBdogeZfVxk&feature=related). Discuss the relationship between the music and the elephants' behavior (e.g., slow moving, repetitive, rhythmic, gentle). • Describe what elephants do when one of their herd is in harm's way. When elephants want to warn others of danger they make what sounds like a shrill trumpet. When an alarm has been sounded, all the elephants form a protective circle around the smaller and younger members of their group. • "Today we are going to read a book about a boy who doesn't know what to do when others use mean words and actions. I want you to think about elephants and how the kids in the story can protect their friends like elephants protect their herd."
Key Vocabulary	**behave, "picking on," bully, tattle/report, narrator** • Review key vocabulary: Inform students, "In this story you may hear a few words that may be unfamiliar to you." Either write words on the chalkboard/whiteboard or type and use word strips. • Show each word (one at a time) and ask, "Who can tell me what this word means?" With student input, briefly define word and use the word in a sentence as an example.
Read the Story	
Post-Reading Discussion	*Review the book—show pictures and ask the following questions:* • Review the first two pages to clearly identify the main characters (*bullies, Ray, narrator, bystanders*). • Which boys do you think are the bullies? How can you tell? • How do you think the narrator feels when he sees Ray being bullied? • How did kids on the playground act like elephants? (*gathered in a circle to protect all members of the herd*) • What mean things did the bullies do and say to Ray?

(continued)

Lesson Plan 3.10
(Continued)

Post-Reading Discussion	• What did the narrator do to help stop the bullying? Did it work?
	• What is the difference between tattling and telling (reporting)?
	• What can you do when you see someone being bullied? You can be like an elephant and:
	    1. Gather in a circle of friends (like the elephants gather their herd).
	    2. Report the bullying (like the elephant, blow a trump of warning). Play an audio file of an elephant trumpeting (http://soundfxcenter.com/sound_effect/search.php?sfx=Elephant).

Extension Activities	**Making an Elephant Trunk** Assist students in making an elephant trunk. The elephant trunk is a reminder for students to (1) gather in a circle and (2) report the bullying so the group can support and help you. An example of making an elephant trunk is found on this Internet website: (http://familycrafts.about.com/od/elephantcrafts/a/ElephantTrunkCraft.htm).
Closure	After the paint on the elephant trunks dries, play "The Elephant" again and let the students act out how they will blow their trumpets when a friend is in danger and how they will gather in a circle to protect each other.

From *Classroom Bullying Prevention, Pre-K–4th Grade: Children's Books, Lesson Plans, and Activities* by Melissa Allen Heath, Tina Taylor Dyches, and Mary Anne Prater. Santa Barbara, CA: Linworth. Copyright © 2013.

The Recess Queen

Author: Alexis O'Neill
Illustrator: Laura Huliska-Beith
Publisher: Scholastic Press
Year: 2002
ISBN: 0-439-20637-5
ISBN 13: 978-0-439-20637-2
Number of Pages: 32 (not paginated)
Reading Level: 2.6 (grade level)
Interest level: PK+

Synopsis: "Mean Jean" bullies classmates and controls the playground. Taller and more aggressive, she wields her power, intimidating everyone during recess. Fearful children avoid her, letting her have her way. Then a new student, teeny tiny Katie Sue, comes to school. Unaware of Mean Jean's playground power, Katie Sue bursts onto the playground and delves into the fun—without Mean Jean's permission! Fearing for Katie Sue, everyone freezes in place. To everyone's— including Mean Jean's—surprise, Katie Sue asks Mean Jean to jump rope with her. On the sideline, a classmate urges, "Go, Jean, go!" So, Jean and Katie Sue start jumping. This new friendship shifts the playground dynamics. From that point forward, no more bullying! Jean joins others in playing and having fun.

Key Characteristics of Book's Characters and Bullying Situation	
Type of Characters	Humans
Bully's Gender, Age, & Race	Female, elementary age, Caucasian
Victim's Gender, Age, & Race	Female, elementary age, Caucasian; classmates (also bullied) represent both genders and a variety of ethnic groups (Caucasian, African American, Latino)
Bully's Age Compared to Victim	Same, but the bully is much bigger
Type of Bullying	Physical, verbal
Location of Bullying	Playground
Victim's Response to Bullying	Bullied classmates are afraid and give in to the bully; new student is not affected
Bully's Response to Bullying	Enjoys taunting and put-downs, gains strength as a ringleader—until new student invites bully to jump rope—then bully stops bullying and joins in jumping rope
Bystander's Response to Bullying	Others avoid and appear fearful of bully; one bystander speaks up and encourages bully to jump rope with victim
Resolution	Bullying stops when Katie Sue ignores Mean Jean's power. Katie Sue freely plays without Mean Jean's permission. Katie Sue invites Mean Jean to play. Shocked to be invited, Mean Jean joins in and actually enjoys herself. Thereafter Jean plays with others and has fun (no more bullying).

Lesson Plan 3.11
The Recess Queen

Book: *The Recess Queen* by Alexis O'Neill, illustrated by Laura Huliska-Beith (2002), Scholastic Press

Reading Level: 2.6 (grade level)
Interest Level: PK+

Lesson Objective(s): To help children play fair and share during recess. After reading this book and discussing the importance of playground rules, each student will identify playground rules that help all students enjoy recess without fear of being bullied.

Materials: Copies of "crown"—one for each student (activity 3.11); crayons or markers to decorate crowns

Pre-Reading Activities	*Show the outside cover of the book and ask the following questions:* • This girl is wearing a crown. What does it mean when someone wears a crown? • Does this "recess queen" look nice and friendly? • What do you think it means to be a "recess queen"? • Do you think this recess queen shares and take turns at recess? Why/why not?
Key Vocabulary	**smoosh, lollapaloosh, kitz and kajammer, puny, loony, dared, gaped, whizzed** • Review key vocabulary: Inform students, "In this story you may hear a few words that may be unfamiliar to you." Either write words on the chalkboard/whiteboard or type and use word strips. • Show each word (one at a time) and ask, "Who can tell me what this word means?" With student input, briefly define word and use the word in a sentence as an example.
Read the Story	
Post-Reading Discussion	*Review the book—show pictures and ask the following questions:* • How would you feel if someone never shared with you, never took turns with you, is always first, and always gets his or her way? • Would you enjoy playing with Mean Jean? • What kind of things did Mean Jean say and do to scare other kids? • Are these students enjoying recess? [*Point to pictures of children reacting to Mean Jean.*] • How are Katie Sue and Mean Jean different from each other? • How was the playground different after Mean Jean and Katie Sue jumped rope together and became friends?
Extension Activities	Kings and queens are powerful people who rule over their kingdoms. Let's pretend that our playground is our kingdom and you are the king or queen of the playground. Let's pretend that everyone must obey your rules. What rules would you make to help kids play nicely with each other—to play fair and share? First, let's talk about playground rules, and then each of you will choose which rules are most important to our playground. When you think of a playground rule, raise your hand and I will call on you to share your idea. I will write your ideas on the chalkboard, and we will choose a couple of rules that we agree to follow. [*Write or draw stick figures on the chalkboard to represent the identified rules. Depending on your students' level of maturity, ask them to pick one, two, or three playground rules.*]

(continued)

From *Classroom Bullying Prevention, Pre-K–4th Grade: Children's Books, Lesson Plans, and Activities* by Melissa Allen Heath, Tina Taylor Dyches, and Mary Anne Prater. Santa Barbara, CA: Linworth. Copyright © 2013.

Extension Activities	**ACTIVITY** • Pass out "crowns" (activity 3.11)—one for each student—and crayons or markers to decorate crowns • Beneath the crown, have the students either print three playground rules or draw pictures to describe the three rules previously discussed. • After writing/drawing playground rules, have students color and decorate their crowns.
Closure	**Write on the board**: *"Play fair and share."* **Explain**: Today we read a story about Mean Jean, the recess queen. Mean Jean—before she meets Katie Sue—is not the type of queen we would want to rule our playground. Our recess will be more fun if we all play fair and share. We need to look out for each other and make sure our playground rules help everyone to have fun. When we see unfair and unkind words and behaviors on the playground, we can speak out against bullying. Although this story has a happy ending, a person like Katie Sue might not be able to stop all bullying. How would you stand up to a bully on the playground? Remember that groups of kids have more power than one student. A group of kids might stand up against the bullying by telling the bully to "Stop it!"

Our Playground Rules

1

_____

2

_____

3

_____

Book Summary 3.12
Say Something

Author: Peggy Moss
Illustrator: Lea Lyon
Publisher: Tilbury House
Year: 2004
ISBN: 0-88448-310X
ISBN 13: 978-0-88448-310-6
Number of Pages: 32 (not paginated)
Reading Level: 2.1 (grade level)
Interest Level: 1+

Synopsis: A young girl describes the types of bullying she sees at school. Although she doesn't participate in the bullying, she remains a silent bystander. When she witnesses bullying on the bus, she doesn't say anything. One day when her friends are not at school, she has to sit alone in the cafeteria and becomes the one who is teased. Upset that other students don't help her, she decides she needs to never again remain silent when witnessing bullying. The next day, she sits on the bus by the girl who is often teased, and they have fun together.

Additional Information: The resolution at the end of the book is not explicitly stated or explained and so this book would require a more in-depth post-reading discussion with younger children. Resources and discussion ideas are included in the back of the book.

Key Characteristics of Book's Characters and Bullying Situation	
Type of Characters	Humans
Bully's Gender, Age, & Race	Mixed, bullies not explicitly depicted
Victim's Gender, Age, & Race	Mixed, elementary age, Caucasian, Asian, African American
Bully's Age Compared to Victim	Same
Type of Bullying	Physical (pushing, throwing things), relational (exclusion), verbal (teasing, name calling, laughing)
Location of Bullying	School yard, hallway, library, bus, cafeteria
Victim's Response to Bullying	Main character observes others being bullied, then is bullied herself; she cries and tells her older brother about bullying; main character resolves to move beyond quietly ignoring (doing nothing), becomes an active bystander
Bully's Response to Bullying	Laughing
Bystander's Response to Bullying	Do nothing; later sits by someone who has been teased and excluded
Resolution	Main character decides to change her response to bullying, sits by girl who was previously excluded

From *Classroom Bullying Prevention, Pre-K–4th Grade: Children's Books, Lesson Plans, and Activities*
by Melissa Allen Heath, Tina Taylor Dyches, and Mary Anne Prater. Santa Barbara, CA: Linworth. Copyright © 2013.

Lesson Plan 3.12
Say Something

Book: *Say Something* by Peggy Moss, illustrated by Lea Lyon (2004), Tilbury House	
Reading Level: 2.1 (grade level) **Interest Level:** 1+	
Lesson Objective(s): Teach students the concept that they can be heroes. They have the power to stop unjust things that they witness. Students will identify three ways they can be a hero when they witness bullying.	
Materials: Chalkboard; pictures of giraffe; giraffe head and neck (activity 3.12—parts 1, 2, 3); scissors; masking tape	
Pre-Reading Activities	• Ask students to describe a "hero." Ask them to tell who their heroes are and write their responses on the board. Emphasize that real heroes are risk takers, people who are not likely to be famous, and who have the courage to help others. • Ask the students what it means to "stick your neck out" to help others (to go out of your way, to be brave). Ask what animal has a long neck (*a giraffe*). Heroes are like giraffes—they stick out their necks to help others. • Looking at the list generated by the students, discuss why those listed are heroes—why they stick their necks out to help others. • Tell the students that they will hear a story about a girl who learns to be brave, to stick her neck out to help those who are bullied.
Key Vocabulary	**hero, "picked on," teased, cafeteria, disappear** • Review key vocabulary: Inform students, "In this story you may hear a few words that may be unfamiliar to you." Either write words on the chalkboard/whiteboard or type and use word strips. • Show each word (one at a time) and ask, "Who can tell me what this word means?" With student input, briefly define word and use the word in a sentence as an example.
Read the Story	
Post-Reading Discussion	*Review the book—show pictures and ask the following questions:* • How can you tell if someone is sad? • How do you think the boy with the glasses feels? • What does the girl telling the story *not do* to the three other students in the story? • What makes the girl cry? What does she wish could happen? • What are all of the other students doing in the cafeteria? What could they have done? • Why does the girl sit with the other girl who always sits alone? What does she learn about her? • What do you think the girl will do about the other two boys being teased? What would you do? • How was the girl in the story like a giraffe—how did she stick her neck out to help others?

(continued)

From *Classroom Bullying Prevention, Pre-K–4th Grade: Children's Books, Lesson Plans, and Activities* by Melissa Allen Heath, Tina Taylor Dyches, and Mary Anne Prater. Santa Barbara, CA: Linworth. Copyright © 2013.

Lesson Plan 3.12
(Continued)

Extension Activities	There are three ways you can be like a giraffe when someone else is being teased or bullied: 1. Say something to the victim. Invite him or her to join your group. 2. Say something to the bully, like, "Stop it"; "I don't want to hear that"; or "Knock it off." 3. Say something to an adult you can trust, like a parent or teacher. Using giraffe head and neck pieces (activity 3.12), make a class giraffe to hang on the wall. Begin with a short neck (just giraffe's head part). Tell the class that when they do something that is sticking their neck out for others, the teacher will add a piece to lengthen the giraffe's neck. Cut neck pieces on the dotted lines and make additional copies as needed to extend the giraffe's neck. Intermittently over the next few weeks, take time to review students' examples of "sticking their necks out" for others who are being bullied.
Closure	Remind students that when they see bullying, they should say something to the person being bullied (supporting them), tell the bully to stop, or tell an adult about the bullying. Each of these responses takes courage.

From *Classroom Bullying Prevention, Pre-K–4th Grade: Children's Books, Lesson Plans, and Activities* by Melissa Allen Heath, Tina Taylor Dyches, and Mary Anne Prater. Santa Barbara, CA: Linworth. Copyright © 2013.

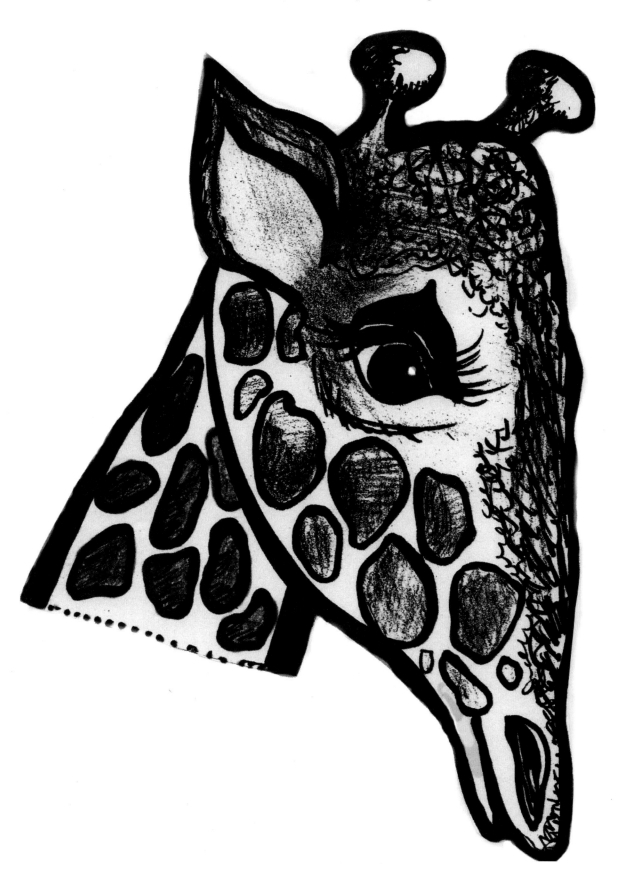

Activity 3.12—part 2 *Say Something*

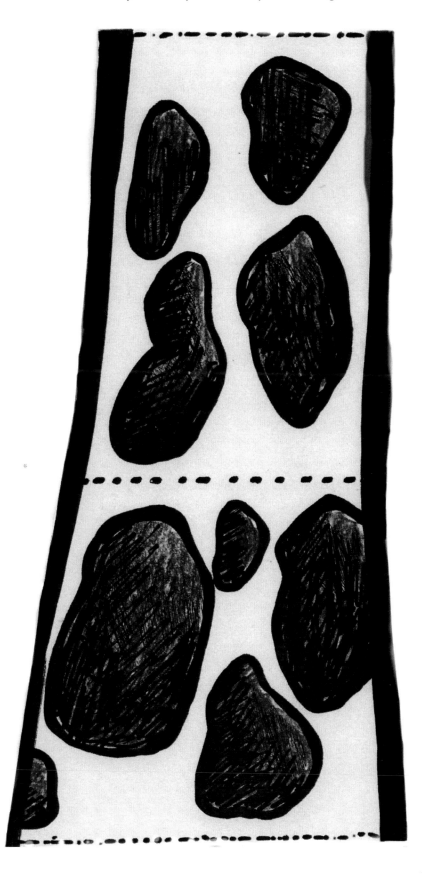

Activity 3.12—part 3 *Say Something*

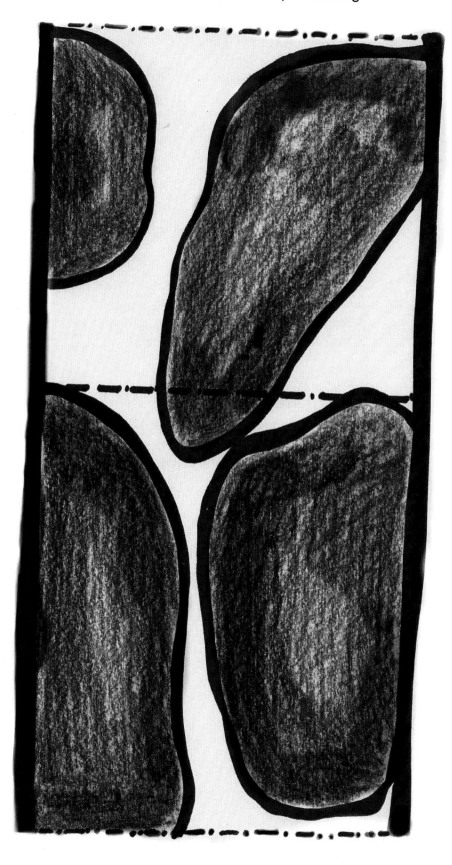

Stand Tall, Molly Lou Melon

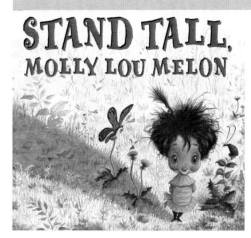

Author: Patty Lovell
Illustrator: David Catrow
Publisher: G. P. Putnam's Sons
Year: 2001
ISBN: 0-399-23416-0
ISBN 13: 978-0-399-23416-3
Number of Pages: 32 (not paginated)
Reading Level: 3.5 (grade level)
Interest Level: PK+

Synopsis: In some ways, Molly Lou Melon is different from other first graders: She is the shortest girl, has buck teeth, has a voice that sounds like "a bullfrog being squeezed by a boa constrictor," and is "fumble fingered." However, she proudly takes her grandmother's advice to believe in herself: "Walk as proudly as you can and the world will look up to you" and "Smile big and the world will smile right alongside you." When Molly Lou Melon moves to a new school, she is teased by Ronald Durkin. Following her grandmother's advice, Molly Lou Melon uses her strengths to score a touchdown, stack pennies on her teeth, and make a large and beautiful snowflake. Impressed, Ronald becomes friends with Molly Lou Melon.

Key Characteristics of Book's Characters and Bullying Situation	
Type of Characters	Humans
Bully's Gender, Age, & Race	Male, elementary age, Caucasian
Victim's Gender, Age, & Race	Female, elementary age, not clearly identified (possibly African American)
Bully's Age Compared to Victim	Same
Type of Bullying	Verbal (name calling)
Location of Bullying	Gym class, outside, in class
Victim's Response to Bullying	Focused on her strengths (which the bully thought were her weaknesses)
Bully's Response to Bullying	Felt foolish, eventually became friends
Bystander's Response to Bullying	Admired the victim
Resolution	Bully is impressed with the victim and becomes friends

Stand Tall, Molly Lou Melon

Book: *Stand Tall, Molly Lou Melon* by Patty Lovell, illustrated by David Catrow (2001), G. P. Putnam's Sons

Reading Level: 3.5 (grade level)
Interest Level: PK+

Lesson Objective(s): To identify personal characteristics that can be viewed as strengths. After listening to the story and answering discussion questions, students will identify characteristics of classmates that they view as strengths, putting a penny in an empty jar for each characteristic they identify. Students will identify three personal characteristics that can be considered strengths and three characteristics of their classmates that can be considered strengths.

Materials: Jar of pennies; empty jar; copies of "I'm Worth a Lot" activity 3.13 handout; pencils/crayons

Pre-Reading Activities	*Show the book's front cover and read the title. Ask the following questions:* • Tell me what you notice about Molly Lou Melon from the book cover. (*She is standing in a patch of weeds, she is only slightly taller than the weeds, her shadow is large, she looks confident.*) • When someone says "stand tall," it can mean to stand upright. What else can it mean? (*confident, brave*) • Can you think of a time when you had to "stand tall" and be confident in yourself? (Have a few students share an experience.) • People who are confident do things that other people might be afraid of doing. Ask the students to repeat this phrase: "So she did." Show the first page in the book where this phrase appears. Write the phrase on the chalkboard and ask students to practice saying this phrase. • Whenever "So she did" is repeated in the book, the point to the phrase and all the students will read it together.
Key Vocabulary	**confident, bullfrog, boa constrictor, "fumble fingered," "shrimpo," glee, worth** • Review key vocabulary: Inform students, "In this story you may hear a few words that may be unfamiliar to you." Either write words on the chalkboard/whiteboard or type and use word strips. • Show each word (one at a time) and ask, "Who can tell me what this word means?" With student input, briefly define word and use the word in a sentence as an example.
Read the Story	
Post-Reading Discussion	*Review the book—show pictures and ask the following questions:* • What clues do you get from the picture of Molly Lou Melon looking outside her bedroom door that she is small? (*tiny pajamas, tiny shoes, ladder by her bed, string to pull lamp switch, small in relation to the cat and balcony*) • How can you tell that Molly Lou Melon is confident? (*standing tall, "My Big Book of Spiders" on the floor*) • Do you think Molly Lou Melon was mad when Ronald Durkin called her "Shrimpo," "Bucky-Tooth Beaver," when he made fun of her voice, and when he told her she made the snowflake "all wrong"? Why/why not?

(continued)

From *Classroom Bullying Prevention, Pre-K–4th Grade: Children's Books, Lesson Plans, and Activities* by Melissa Allen Heath, Tina Taylor Dyches, and Mary Anne Prater. Santa Barbara, CA: Linworth. Copyright © 2013.

Lesson Plan 3.13
(Continued)

Post-Reading Discussion	• Why do you think Molly Lou Melon followed her grandma's advice? What do you notice about her grandma? (*She is tiny like Molly Lou Melon.*)
	• Remind students that Molly Lou Melon didn't believe what Ronald Durkin thought about her. She saw her strengths, not her weaknesses.
	   ○ Because she was short, she could run under the legs of Ronald Durkin and score a touchdown.
	   ○ Because she had buck teeth, she could stack 10 pennies on her teeth.
	   ○ Because she had a voice like a bullfrog, she used that clear and strong voice to show her strength to Ronald.
	   ○ Because she believed in herself, she made the most beautiful snowflake of all.

Extension Activities	Show a penny and ask what it is worth. Show a jar of pennies and have them estimate how much it is worth. When many pennies are put together, they are worth a lot. Use accompanying activity 3.13 ("I'm Worth a Lot"). For each penny on the handout, have the students write or draw one personal characteristic that could be considered a weakness, and then describe how it can be viewed as a strength.
Closure	Encourage students to be aware of their classmates' strengths. Ask students to watch for others doing something nice for another student, doing a good job with their schoolwork, or doing anything else that shows their strengths. Ask students to remember these examples. At the end of the day, take five minutes for students to share these examples with the class. Ask them to describe what they noticed about their classmates. For each strength that a student notices, they will take a penny from the class jar and place it in the empty jar. As the jar fills, classmates will monitor the pennies in the jar, noting that the once-empty jar is now worth a lot more!

I'm Worth a Lot

	Something about Me	How It Makes Me Worth a Lot

Image retrieved from Microsoft Clipart

Book Summary 3.14
Yoon and the Jade Bracelet

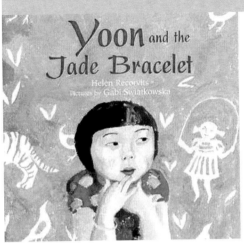

Author: Helen Recorvits
Illustrator: Gabi Swiatkowska
Publisher: Farrar, Straus, Giroux
Year: 2008
ISBN: 0-374-38689-7
ISBN 13: 978-0-374-38689-4
Number of Pages: 32 (not paginated)
Reading Level: 2.9 (grade level)
Interest Level: PK+
Available in Spanish: *Yoon y la Pulsera de Jade*

Synopsis: New to her school, Yoon watches other girls play jump rope during recess. Although she wants a jump rope for her birthday, she receives a jade bracelet and a book about a girl outwitting a tiger. Her mother explains the carving inside the bracelet—Korean symbols for Yoon's name, "Shining Wisdom." During recess an older girl bribes Yoon into letting her wear the bracelet, because that is what "friends" do. The older girl refuses to return the bracelet. Noticing Yoon's sadness, the teacher elicits an explanation. The teacher brings the older girl into Yoon's classroom and the older girl denies taking the bracelet. However, classmates support Yoon's story. Then Yoon explains the bracelet's engraving. The older girl has no idea what the engraving represents. Caught in deception, the older girl returns Yoon's jade bracelet.

Key Characteristics of Book's Characters and Bullying Situation	
Type of Characters	Humans
Bully's Gender, Age, & Race	Female, elementary age, Caucasian
Victim's Gender, Age, & Race	Female, elementary age, Korean
Bully's Age Compared to Victim	Older
Type of Bullying	Relational (manipulation); taking and not returning jade bracelet; ignoring pleas to return bracelet; dishonest to maintain control
Location of Bullying	Playground
Victim's Response to Bullying	Being nice; letting bully have her way; asking for return of bracelet; reporting incident to teacher, including details about engraving inside the bracelet
Bully's Response to Bullying	When confronted by the teacher, the bully lies about Yoon's bracelet, claiming it is her own
Bystander's Response to Bullying	Initially no support; when teacher confronts the bully, classmates support Yoon's side of the story
Resolution	With teacher's assistance, older girl returns Yoon's bracelet

Lesson Plan 3.14
Yoon and the Jade Bracelet

Book: *Yoon and the Jade Bracelet* by Helen Recorvits, illustrated by Gabi Swiatkowska (2008), Farrar, Straus, and Giroux

Reading Level: 2.9 (grade level)
Interest Level: PK+

Lesson Objective(s): To teach children the following points: (1) True friends do not take advantage of each other and (2) When students cannot independently work through bullying situations, they can speak up for each other and—if needed—ask an adult for help. After hearing the story, students will make a friendship bracelet, stringing three green beads on a string, representing three symbols: (a) happiness and hope—true friendship brings happiness; (b) friends include others; and (c) friends and teachers "take a stand," "step in" and "speak up" to help when someone is taking advantage of a classmate.

Materials: Green plastic beads (three for each student); 11" piece of green yarn (one for each student); copies of activity 3.14 for each student; tracing paper or wax paper (one piece for each student); and pencil (one for each student)—younger students trace the handout's tiger and older students trace the handout's Korean symbols.

Pre-Reading Activities	*Review the book—show pictures and ask the following questions:* • This is a story about a girl, Yoon, who used to live in Korea, a country far away. [*Show location on map.*] She moved to the United States just before her birthday. She wanted a jump rope for her birthday. • Guess what Yoon might be thinking about in this picture. [*Show students the front cover of the book.*] • The name of this story is *Yoon and the Jade Bracelet.* [*Show students the front cover of the book.*] Look at Yoon's bracelet. What color is Yoon's bracelet? What is the bracelet made of? Have you ever received a special gift such as a ring or bracelet?
Key Vocabulary	**disappointment, jade, gem, tricked, trickster, etched, symbol, wisdom, shame, courage** • Review key vocabulary: Inform students, "In this story you may hear a few words that may be unfamiliar to you." Either write words on the chalkboard/whiteboard or type and use word strips. • Show each word (one at a time) and ask, "Who can tell me what this word means?" With student input, briefly define word and use the word in a sentence as an example.
Read the Story	
Post-Reading Discussion	*Review the book—show pictures and ask the following questions:* • Yoon is a new student at this school. How does Yoon feel when she sees everyone jumping rope at recess? • Why did Yoon feel "tricked by a tiger"? • When Yoon came home from school, why didn't she tell her mother about the older girl who took the jade bracelet? • How did the teacher know something was wrong with Yoon? • Why did the teacher bring the older girl into Yoon's classroom?

(continued)

Lesson Plan 3.14
(*Continued*)

Post-Reading Discussion	• How did Yoon's classmates help the teacher learn the true story about the bracelet and who it really belonged to? • How did the teacher prove the bracelet was Yoon's? What was on the inside of the bracelet?

Extension Activities	**Role-Play**
	
	• Act out a role-play. We will change this story about Yoon to show what we would do. In our story, we will step in when the older girl takes Yoon's bracelet. We will speak up and say something to the older girl. What could we say? [*Wait for students to offer ideas.*] In our role-play when the older girl takes the bracelet, two girls and two boys will speak up for Yoon.
	• [*Assign these parts and suggest what they might say.*] Tell the older girl: "True friends do not take their friends' things. Give the bracelet back to Yoon." [*Suggest one girl invite Yoon to jump rope with their group of friends.*] "I want you to come and jump rope with our group. You can join in with us."
	
	Friendship Bracelet
	
	• Many years ago, friendship bracelets were made by Native Americans in Central and South America. Today we follow their tradition; one friend ties a bracelet onto their friend's wrist as they make a wish. The friend wears the bracelet until it is worn out and falls off. The moment the bracelet falls off, the friend's wish comes true.
	• Although this "wish-making" is make-believe, our class is making bracelets today to remind us about three things. Each green bead will help us to remember:
	  ○ (1) True Friendship: Green is a symbol of happiness and hope—true friendship brings happiness.
	  ○ (2) Include Others: Friends invite others to join in the fun so everyone feels included.
	  ○ (3) Speak Up: We (as friends and teacher) take a stand, step in, and speak up when someone is being dishonest and taking advantage of another student.
	• String beads on 11" piece of green yarn, tie on each student's wrist—not too tight. Remind students about what each bead stands for.
	
	Activity 3.14 "Yoon and the Jade Bracelet"
	
	• Pass out the "Yoon and the Jade Bracelet" handout.
	• Hand out wax paper or tracing paper, and a pencil for each student.
	• Read the handout aloud.
	• Explain how to trace on waxed paper or on tracing paper. Have students trace the tiger and/or the traditional Korean symbols.
	• Encourage students to think about Yoon's story and how they would show their courage if they were one of Yoon's classmates.

Closure	**Write on the board:** *"True Friend"* **Explain:** Today's story was about Yoon, a new student who was shy. An older student acted like she was a friend, but she took Yoon's special jade bracelet and would not give it back. Other students saw what was happening but did not speak up until the teacher asked questions. We can join others into our group. We can be true friends. We can speak up when classmates need us. When we need an adult, we can talk with our teacher and he/she will help us.

Yoon and the Jade Bracelet

- **True friendship brings happiness.**
- **True friends include others in the fun.**
- **True friends have courage to speak up when someone is bullied.**

友	Koreans use picture words, not letters of the alphabet. This traditional Korean picture word means "friend." True friendship brings happiness. True friends include others.
智	This is a traditional Korean symbol for "wisdom." Wisdom means using our knowledge (what we know) in the right place, in the right way, and at the right time. It takes wisdom to protect yourself and friends from bullies.
勇氣	These two traditional picture words mean bravery within your heart and mind: "courage." When someone is being bullied, it takes courage to **TAKE A STAND**, **STEP IN**, and **SPEAK UP**.

Book Summary 3.15
Don't Laugh at Me

Authors: Steve Seskin and Allen Shamblin
Illustrator: Glin Dibley
Publisher: Tricycle Press
Year: 2002
ISBN: 1-582-46058-2
ISBN 13: 978-1-582-46058-1
Number of Pages: 32 (not paginated)
Reading Level: 1.6 (grade level)
Interest Level: K+
Available in Spanish: *No Te Rias de Mi*

Synopsis: This book identifies a wide variety of children who are teased, left out, and ridiculed. These individuals include a boy who wears glasses, a girl with braces, a boy who is chosen last on the playground, and a boy who is slower than others in his class. The repeated themes are simply, "Don't laugh at me"; "Don't call me names"; and "Don't get your pleasure from my pain." The book emphasizes that although each of us is unique in some way, no one should be bullied, because we are all different.

Additional Information: This book is accompanied by a CD including the lyrical and instrumental versions of the song "Don't Laugh at Me." Additionally, several excellent videos with music (Don't Laugh at Me) are available on YouTube:

- http://www.youtube.com/watch?v=HTNVXlirF4Y [This video uses pictures from the book]
- http://www.youtube.com/watch?v=7jNV6dn3YvQ [Peter Yarrow (solo) singing]
- http://www.youtube.com/watch?v=FVjbo8dW9c8&feature=fvwrel [Mark Wills (country western)]

Key Characteristics of Book's Characters and Bullying Situation	
Type of Characters	Humans
Bully's Gender, Age, & Race	Various
Victim's Gender, Age, & Race	Various
Bully's Age Compared to Victim	Varied
Type of Bullying	Relational, verbal
Location of Bullying	Varied
Victim's Response to Bullying	Sadness, exclusion
Bully's Response to Bullying	Not clearly depicted
Bystander's Response to Bullying	Not clearly depicted
Resolution	Not clearly depicted

Lesson Plan 3.15
Don't Laugh at Me

Book: *Don't Laugh at Me* by Steve Seskin and Allen Shamblin, illustrated by Glin Dibley (2002), Tricycle Press

Reading Level: 1.6 (grade level)
Interest Level: K+

Lesson Objective(s): To increase students' awareness of name calling and verbal bullying in school. Students will identify names that are respectful and those that are put-downs. They will identify ways to help others who are called names.

Materials: Two apples; knife for cutting the apples; "Don't Laugh at Me" CD (or YouTube videos or MP3 file); copies of activity 3.15, Respectful Names handout (one for each student discussion dyad)

Pre-Reading Activities	• Have students sit in a circle. Ask the students, "Have you ever heard someone make fun of someone else by calling them a name? We call this 'name calling' or 'put-downs.' How do people feel when they are put down like this?" • Share an experience when you were called a name. "When I was called this name, I felt bad. It's like the apple is being dropped down to the ground (drop the apple). Now, I will pass the apple around to you who want to share a time when you saw someone say something unkind to you or someone else." Then drop the apple and pass it to the next child who wants to share a story. Ask each student who shares a story is asked to drop the apple. • Show the other apple. "This apple has been treated kindly." Share an example of how you felt when someone said something nice to you. "If you have a story to share about a time when someone said something nice to you, then we will gently pass the apple to you." • When we say unkind things to other people, it hurts. Although we might not be able to see the hurt on the outside, on the inside they are bruised. [*Cut open the first apple and show the bruises.*] • When we are kind to each other, it is respectful. [*Cut open the second apple, slicing the apple at the midsection to reveal a "star" configuration in the seeds.*] When we use respectful words, we are stars, just like in this apple. (Idea from http://kamaron.org/.)
Key Vocabulary	**geek, braces, beggar, stare, deaf, blind** • Review key vocabulary: Inform students, "In this story you may hear a few words that may be unfamiliar to you." Either write words on the chalkboard/whiteboard or type and use word strips. • Show each word (one at a time) and ask, "Who can tell me what this word means?" With student input, briefly define word and use the word in a sentence as an example.
Read the Story	

Post-Reading Discussion	*Review the book—show pictures and ask the following questions:*
	
	• After reading the story, play the song "Don't Laugh at Me," available on CD, on YouTube, and on the Operation Respect website.
	   ○ Video http://www.youtube.com/watch?v=HTNVXlirF4Y
	   ○ mp3 http://www.operationrespect.org/curricula/EnglishDLAM.mp3
	• As the music plays, show the book's illustrations.

(continued)

Lesson Plan 3.15
(Continued)

Extension Activities	• Have students pair up to ask each other the discussion questions found on the "Respectful Names" handout (activity 3.15). 1. What are good names that you like to be called? 2. What are bad names or put-downs that you *don't* like to be called? 3. How can you make someone feel better after he or she has been called a name? 4. What can you do when you hear someone call another child a name? • Following the paired discussion, ask students to share their responses with the whole group. • Collect students' papers.
Closure	Some people say that "Sticks and stones may break my bones, but words will never hurt me." But we know this is not true. [*Show the bruised apple.*] Just like a dropped apple is bruised inside, when people call us names, we can be bruised and hurt inside. When we choose to use respectful language with each other, we will feel better inside and others will feel better too.

Respectful Names Discussion Questions

1. What are **good** names that you like to be called?

2. What are **bad** names or put-downs that you don't like to be called?

3. How can you make someone **feel better** after he or she has been called a name?

4. What **can you do** when you hear someone call another child a name?

Respectful Names Discussion Questions

1. What are **good** names that you like to be called?

2. What are **bad** names or put-downs that you don't like to be called?

3. How can you make someone **feel better** after he or she has been called a name?

4. What **can you do** when you hear someone call another child a name?

Chapter 4

LESSON PLANS TO INCREASE SUPPORT FOR VULNERABLE STUDENTS

Bullies target students for a wide variety of reasons, but they generally victimize students who appear different from what is considered "normal." This includes students who are emotionally and/or physically vulnerable, small, weak, shy, quiet, anxious, hypervigilant, easily agitated, sensitive, and so forth. In other words, students may be bullied for almost any unique characteristic. In particular, physical weakness is identified as the most consistent predictor of victimization (Olweus, 1993; Rose, Monda-Amaya, & Espelage, 2011). Other characteristics commonly include differences in height, weight, race, wearing glasses or braces, and so forth. Because bullies tend to victimize peers who appear physically or socially different, students with disabilities are especially vulnerable (Rose et al., 2011). Although this chapter focuses on the vulnerability of students with disabilities, the information is also applicable to other vulnerable groups.

Educational Disabilities

Approximately 13 percent of students in the United States are identified with an educational disability and receive special education services. The most common disabilities include specific learning disabilities, speech/language impairments, developmental delays, intellectual disability, emotional disturbance, other health impairments, and autism. Students may also be identified with lower-incidence disabilities, such as hearing impairments, orthopedic impairments, visual impairments, multiple disabilities, deaf-blindness, and traumatic brain injury.

Unfortunately, because students identified with disabilities are formally labeled by the U.S. educational system and receive services through special education, the traditional education structure of American schools may inadvertently contribute to bullying. After reviewing research studies that investigated perpetrated bullying and victimization of students identified as having educational disabilities, Rose et al. (2011) summarized key findings. Their findings indicate that compared to nondisabled peers, a greater proportion of students identified with disabilities and special needs—over 50 percent—are targeted by bullies. Similar to mainstream bullying, bullying of students served in special education includes name calling and teasing, physical aggression, and social exclusion.

Student Vulnerabilities

Rose et al. (2011) indicated that students were considered especially vulnerable to bullying if they received special education services in resource rooms and self-contained settings. In particular, separating students from mainstream settings increased the likelihood of social exclusion, further highlighting differences between students. During the 2008–2009 school year, approximately 60 percent of students identified with disabilities spent 80 percent or more of their time in general classes; the remaining 40 percent spent less than 80 percent of their time in general classes. Approximately 15 percent of students in special education (those with more severe disabilities) spent 60 percent or more of their time in special education settings (U.S. Department of Education, National Center for Education Statistics, 2010).

Another aspect of American schools that creates divisiveness is the entrenched competition promoted by schools. School competitions emphasize desired athletic and academic abilities while simultaneously disregarding other student abilities. Typically struggling with academic achievement and/or challenged with physical limitations, students with disabilities may have limited opportunities to associate with same-age peers in competitive academic settings or to participate in sports and school clubs. Although unintended, this type of competition and the exclusion of students with disabilities perpetuates barriers and misunderstandings between students in special education and students in general education.

Rose et al. (2011) also indicated that in comparison to nondisabled peers, a higher proportion of students with disabilities perpetrate bullying. Additionally, students with disabilities may be drawn into bullying situations because they want to "fit in" with their peers. Furthermore, students with disabilities may have limited awareness regarding the impact of bullying and how their behavior may be perceived by others (Hoover & Stenhjem, 2003). Consequently, vulnerable students require additional supervision to ensure their safety and the safety of others. This is particularly true in less-supervised settings, such as school cafeterias, bathrooms, hallways, and before and after school—including school bus transportation and walking to and from school.

Students identified with disabilities, particularly those identified with emotional disturbance (emotional/behavioral disorders), are more prone to exhibit aggressive behaviors. Aggressive behaviors and feelings of disconnectedness from school ultimately contribute to school dropout (Coie, 2004). Over half of students identified with emotional disturbance (ED) never graduate from high school (Cobb, Sample, Alwell, & Johns, 2006). In particular many students identified with disabilities experience increased emotional and behavioral volatility, discord in peer relationships, and have difficulties maintaining supportive personal relationships across the lifespan (Hoover & Stenhjem, 2003).

Supporting Vulnerable Students with Bibliotherapy

To counter these negative prognoses, bibliotherapy offered in early elementary school has the potential to strengthen positive student–student and student–adult relationships. In turn, these positive relationships strengthen children's resiliency and increase feelings of connectedness to peers, teachers, and school (Johnson, 2008).

In order to better support students identified with disabilities, we propose bibliotherapy as a strategy to address common challenges identified in the research literature (Rose et al., 2011). Though focusing on children's special needs, optimally these selected stories should be shared with all children, those served in general and special education. All children benefit from these basic lessons and opportunities to practice social skills and better understand emotions that underlie behavior.

The following suggestions will assist us in using bibliotherapy to support students who may be more vulnerable to being bullied.

- Because children with disabilities often misinterpret social cues, the educator should read stories that model social skills. Take additional time to explain and role-play appropriate social interactions.

- Children identified with special education needs may have difficulties controlling impulsivity and aggression, particularly when physical, social, and emotional needs are not being met. Children may also become aggressive when they feel threatened. When reading stories, invite students to identify feelings and frustrations, helping them better understand their own feelings and others' feelings. Role-play appropriate ways to respond to these feelings.

- Children with disabilities may have limited opportunities to interact with peers and to develop social connectedness. Offer supervised opportunities and encourage interactions between students in general and special education settings. Help students find common ground and shared interests. Read stories that model respect for individual differences and demonstrate patience and kindness.

- Students with disabilities may lack assertion skills and need to be coached in saying, "No, stop it!" Read stories that model appropriate self-assertion skills. Role-play interactions and practice these skills.

- Use stories to help inform students about disabilities and appropriate ways to interact with students who may look or act differently. This is an important part of education, helping us interact comfortably and respectfully with others.

Table 4.1
Chapter 4: Books and Core Messages

Book	Core Message
Be Good to Eddie Lee	Even though others may look different, we can be friends. Everyone has something to teach us.
My Sister, Alicia Mae	We must step in and speak up when we see someone treating someone unkindly. This is especially important when this person is smaller and weaker.
Keeping Up with Roo	When someone is not included, he or she might feel left out and sad. We must be thoughtful of others' feelings and find ways to include them in the fun.
Thank You, Mr. Falker	Our words and our actions affect how others feel about themselves.
Crow Boy	When someone looks and acts differently than others, he or she is often left out and bullied. We must include everyone and treat everyone with respect.

As a quick overview of the five lesson plans included in this chapter, Table 4.1 succinctly summarizes each book's core message. Additionally, each lesson plan provides basic information, including the book's title, author, illustrator (if different from the author), publisher, year of publication, ISBN identifiers, number of pages and if the book is paginated, reading level (by grade and month), and estimated interest level. A brief synopsis of the story highlights the plot and resolution to bullying situations. Additional information describes supplementary resources included in the book. Descriptions of characters and bullying situations are listed in a table preceding each lesson plan. These descriptions include the type of character (e.g., animal or human); gender, age, and race of bully and victim; age difference between bully and victim; type of bullying; location of bullying; victim's response to bullying; bully's response to bullying; bystanders' response to bullying; and resolution of bullying. This information gives a quick synopsis of important details to consider when selecting books to share with children.

Similar to the previous chapter, each lesson plan in Chapter 4 includes the following ingredients: (a) descriptive information (book title, author and illustrator, year of publication, and publisher); (b) reading level and interest level; (c) lesson objectives; (d) materials needed to teach lesson; (e) pre-reading activities (questions to stimulate interest and discussion); (f) key vocabulary; (g) read the story; (h) post-reading discussion; (i) extension activities; and (j) closure. By following the outlines, educators are able to present lesson plans with minimal preparation.

Book Summary 4.1
Be Good to Eddie Lee

Author: Virginia Fleming
Illustrator: Floyd Cooper
Publisher: Philomel Books
Year: 1993, 1997
ISBN: 0-698-11582-1
ISBN 13: 978-0-698-11582-8
Number of Pages: 32 (unpaginated)
Reading Level: 3.6 (grade level)
Interest Level: K+

Synopsis: Christy's mother tells her to be nice to Eddie Lee because he's lonesome and different. Christy and JimBud run off to the lake, ignoring Eddie Lee as he follows them. They tell him to stay home, hurting his feelings. But he continues following them to the lake. To catch a salamander, he jumps into the lake, splashing the other children. Unable to reach a lily in the middle of the lake, he shows Christy another pond with lilies and frog eggs. Christy wants to take the frog eggs home, but Eddie Lee tells her not to. Christy figures out that the frog eggs will die if removed from the pond. When they see their reflections in the pond with ripples distorting their faces, Eddie Lee tells her she looks funny—but that's okay because it's what's here (as he touches his chest) that counts.

Key Characteristics of Book's Characters and Bullying Situation	
Type of Characters	Humans
Bully's Gender, Age, & Race	Male and female, elementary age, Caucasian
Victim's Gender, Age, & Race	Male, elementary age, Caucasian
Bully's Age Compared to Victim	Same
Type of Bullying	Name calling, ignoring
Location of Bullying	Outside during summer play
Victim's Response to Bullying	Hurt feelings
Bully's Response to Bullying	One leaves, the other learns the victim has a lot to offer
Bystander's Response to Bullying	None
Resolution	One bully and victim appear to become friends

Lesson Plan 4.1
Be Good to Eddie Lee

Book: *Be Good to Eddie Lee* by Virginia Fleming, illustrated by Floyd Cooper (1993, 1997), Philomel Books

Reading Level: 3.6 (grade level)
Interest Level: K+

Lesson Objective(s): To teach that even though others may look different they can be friends and teach us something. After listening to the story, students will write down several things that they do well.

Materials: Digital camera; color printer to print photographs; bucket of water; large paper; crayons or markers; poster of Emerson quote

Pre-Reading Activities	• Ask students what they do during the summer. • Tell them they will be reading a story about three children—Christy, Eddie Lee, and JimBud—and what they do in the summer. • Show the book's front cover and read the title. Ask for students' opinions about why the book is titled *Be Good to Eddie Lee*. Ask students what type of flower he has in his hand. [*Answer: lily*]
Key Vocabulary	**lonesome, waddled, ignored, kingfisher, hatched, whopper, salamander, quiver, water lilies, tadpoles, reflection** • Review key vocabulary: Inform students, "In this story you may hear a few words that may be unfamiliar to you." Either write words on the chalkboard/whiteboard or type and use word strips. • Show each word (one at a time) and ask, "Who can tell me what this word means?" With student input, briefly define word and use the word in a sentence as an example.
Read the Story	
Post-Reading Discussion	*Review the book—show pictures and ask the following questions:* • Why didn't Christie and JimBud want to play with Eddie Lee? • Would you want to play with him? Why/why not? • How do Christie and JimBud make Eddie Lee feel? Why? • What does Eddie Lee know how to do that the others don't know how to do? • Why do you think JimBud doesn't want to go with Christie and Eddie Lee? • What do Christie and Eddie Lee find at the pond? • How did Christie know what Eddie Lee was trying to say? • What makes their faces look funny in the water? • What does Eddie Lee mean by "It's what's here that counts"? • Do you think Eddie Lee and Christie continue to play in the summer? Why/why not? • Do you think JimBud joins them? Why/why not? • Discuss with students the differences between how we look on the outside and how we feel on the inside. Ask them if they would feel differently on the inside if they looked differently on the outside. Explore why or why not. Emphasize that who we are on the inside doesn't change how we look on the outside. • Discuss how we shouldn't treat others differently by the way that they look on the outside. Review the story for how Christie and JimBud make Eddie Lee feel badly.

(continued)

Lesson Plan 4.1
(Continued)

Extension Activities	• Remind students that Eddie Lee says that it's what's inside that counts. Display a poster with the printed quote: "**What lies behind us and what lies before us are small matters compared to what lies within us**" (Ralph Waldo Emerson). Explain what is meant by "lies behind us," "lies before us," and "lies within us." • Tell students that they are going to have their pictures taken two ways; one will be a "regular" picture of their face. The second picture will be taken of their reflection in water that has a ripple. Take the photos. • Give students a large rectangular piece of paper. Have them fold them in thirds lengthwise. In the middle ask students to write words describing things they do well. If necessary, provide a list of examples from which they can choose (e.g., playing baseball, reading, cleaning up, helping my mom, drawing, singing). • Once the photographs are printed, have students glue them on the first and last third of their paper. Post the pictures on the bulletin board with the Emerson quotation.
Closure	Remind students that the two pictures of themselves are reminders that what counts is what's on the inside of a person and those who may look or act differently should not be treated differently.

Book Summary 4.2
My Sister, Alicia May

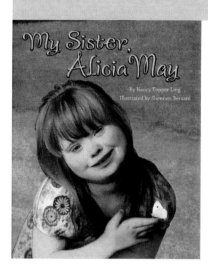

Author: Nancy Tupper Ling
Illustrator: Shennen Bersani
Publisher: Pleasant St. Press
Year: 2009
ISBN: 0-9792035-9-7
ISBN 13: 978-0-9792035-9-6
Number of Pages: 28
Reading Level: 2 (grade level)
Interest Level: PK+

Synopsis: Rachel thinks her younger sister, Alicia May, is special in many ways: She likes many things other children like, and she also loves bugs and watches them closely—even counting the dots on ladybugs. Transitions are hard for Alicia May. After playing with Katie and Rachel at Katie's home, Alicia May wants to stay and play with the train instead of going home. Katie lets her take the caboose, which makes her happy again. Sometimes Alicia May annoys Rachel, and she gets tired of watching out for her. The first three days they ride the school bus together, a group of boys are mean to Alicia May. At first Katie and Rachel pretend they don't know her. But on the third day, Rachel tells the boys to "Knock it off!" They stop bullying Alicia May.

Additional Information: Based on the illustrator's notes and the illustrations, Alicia May has Down syndrome. The illustrator indicates that she received this assignment without the editor knowing that she had a younger sister with Down syndrome and found a "kindred spirit" in Rachel.

Key Characteristics of Book's Characters and Bullying Situation	
Type of Characters	Humans
Bully's Gender, Age, & Race	Male, elementary age, Caucasian
Victim's Gender, Age, & Race	Female, elementary age, Caucasian
Bully's Age Compared to Victim	Same
Type of Bullying	Telling the victim what to do and say
Location of Bullying	School bus
Victim's Response to Bullying	Unclear
Bully's Response to Bullying	Bullies stop
Bystander's Response to Bullying	Ignored, then told them to "Knock it off!"
Resolution	Bullies stop telling her what to do and say

Lesson Plan 4.2
My Sister, Alicia May

Book: *My Sister, Alicia May* by Nancy Tupper Ling, illustrated by Shennen Bersani (2009), Pleasant St. Press

Reading Level: 2 (grade level)
Interest Level: PK+

Lesson Objective(s): To teach students to stand up when they see or hear bullying. After listening to the story, students will learn the song "Stand Up" and commit to stand up when they see or hear someone being mean to another student.

Materials: Music to "Farmer in the Dell" and instrument, if accompaniment is desired

Pre-Reading Activities	• Ask students if they have a younger brother or sister and whether they enjoy playing with them. • Tell them they will be reading a story about Alicia May, who is Rachel's little sister. Sometimes Rachel enjoys playing with Alicia May and sometimes she finds her annoying. • Show the front cover and read the title.
Key Vocabulary	**astronaut, polka dots, notices, caboose, "sharp memory," forever, annoy** • Review key vocabulary: Inform students, "In this story you may hear a few words that may be unfamiliar to you." Either write words on the chalkboard/whiteboard or type and use word strips. • Show each word (one at a time) and ask, "Who can tell me what this word means?" With student input, briefly define word and use the word in a sentence as an example.
Read the Story	
Post-Reading Discussion	*Review the book—show pictures and ask the following questions:* • Why do you think Rachel thinks Alicia May is special? • Do you like dogs and horses like Alicia May? • How many dots do you think ladybugs have on their backs? • Why doesn't Alicia May want to leave Katie's house? • How did Katie make her feel better about going home? • Why do you think Alicia May calls her sister Rae-Rae? • What does Alicia May remember to do? What do you remember to do? • Why doesn't Rachel always play with Alicia May? • Why does Rachel sometimes think Alicia May is annoying? • What did the boys on the bus do? • How did it make Rachel feel? How do you think it made Alicia May feel? • What did Rachel do about the boys?
Extension Activities	**Song Activity** • Tell students that they are going to learn a new song. The song will tell them what to do when they see someone hurting someone else. Just like Rachel, who told the boys on the bus to stop telling her sister what to say and do, we all need to stand up when others are being mean.

(continued)

Lesson Plan 4.2

(Continued)

Extension Activities	• Teach them the following song set to the music of "Farmer in the Dell." When they sing the words "stand up," they can physically stand up and then sit down again until they get to the next verse.
	• Discuss with students how to "tell others not to be bad," what "hearing names" might sound like, and what "someone being mean" might look and sound like. Emphasize that "stand up" means to tell others not to be mean.
	  ○ Stand up when you see sad.
	    Tell others not to be bad.
	    Short or tall or weak or small,
	    It's time we all are glad.
	  ○ Stand up when you hear names.
	    It's not like playing games.
	    Short or tall or weak or small,
	    We all are much the same.
	  ○ Stand up when someone's mean.
	    Tell others what you've seen.
	    Short or tall or weak or small,
	    We know not to be mean.
	  ○ Stand up when others cry.
	    And ask them to tell why.
	    Short or tall or weak or small,
	    Let's all give it a try.

Closure	Remind students that in the story, Rachel stood up for her sister, Alicia May. If necessary, retell that portion of the story. Tell them that when they see someone being hurt that they should remember the song they learned and to "stand up" for the hurt person.

Book Summary 4.3
Keeping Up with Roo

Author: Sharlee Glenn
Illustrator: Dan Andreasen
Publisher: G. P. Putnam's Sons
Year: 2004
ISBN: 0399234802
Number of Pages: 32
Reading Level: 4.1 (estimated)
Interest Level: K+

Synopsis: Gracie is best friends with Roo, Gracie's aunt with intellectual disabilities. As a young child, Gracie played with Roo all over the farm. They played school and Roo taught Gracie basic reading and math skills. But once Gracie starts attending real school, she leaves Roo behind. Now, their differences are more noticeable. One day Gracie brings her friend Sarah home. Roo is dressed funny with long green and purple ribbons in her hair. Sarah asks who this strangely dressed person is. Embarrassed, Gracie tells Sarah that Roo is "nobody." They exclude Roo from their play. However, Gracie gradually recognizes the many things Roo has taught her. She tells Sarah she needs to introduce her to someone, her aunt Roo. Then Gracie insists they play school, with Roo as the teacher and Gracie and Sarah the students.

Key Characteristics of Book's Characters and Bullying Situation	
Type of Characters	Humans
Bully's Gender, Age, & Race	Female, elementary age, Caucasian
Victim's Gender, Age, & Race	Female, adult with disability, Caucasian
Bully's Age Compared to Victim	Younger
Type of Bullying	Relational (ignoring)
Location of Bullying	At home
Victim's Response to Bullying	Sadness
Bully's Response to Bullying	Sadness, not hungry
Bystander's Response to Bullying	Eventually accepts the victim as a playmate
Resolution	Bully recognizes what she has learned from the victim

From *Classroom Bullying Prevention, Pre-K–4th Grade: Children's Books, Lesson Plans, and Activities* by Melissa Allen Heath, Tina Taylor Dyches, and Mary Anne Prater. Santa Barbara, CA: Linworth. Copyright © 2013.

Lesson Plan 4.3
Keeping Up with Roo

Book: *Keeping Up with Roo* by Sharlee Glenn, illustrated by Dan Andreasen (2004), G. P. Putnam's Sons

Reading Level: 4.1 (estimated)
Interest Level: K+

Lesson Objective(s): To teach the importance of appreciating all people, especially those who are different. After listening to the story, students act out the story line, differentiating between what Gracie did that made Roo happy and what she did that made Roo sad.

Materials: Cardstock, red and blue crayons, scissors, two Popsicle/craft sticks for each student, tape, one set of stick faces for the teacher (may wish to make them larger)

Pre-Reading Activities	• Ask students if they like to play school. When they do, who gets to be the teacher and who is the student? • Show the picture on the cover and tell them the title. Ask them who they think Roo is. Explain it is the lady in overalls with funny hair and the girl's name is Gracie. • State: "This story is about Gracie and Roo. Roo is Gracie's aunt. Who has an aunt? Does anyone have an aunt named Roo? Roo is a short name for the name Ruth. Sometimes Roo and Gracie play school just like you."
Key Vocabulary	**swoop, quiver, flung, pumping, version, "Stars and Stripes Forever," wake, adventures, tart, corral, sprained, water skeeters, apple crates, willow switch, crossroads, overalls, experimenting, fluttered, abandoned, May pole, drizzled, reruns** • Review key vocabulary: Inform students, "In this story you may hear a few words that may be unfamiliar to you." Either write words on the chalkboard/whiteboard or type and use word strips. • Show each word (one at a time) and ask, "Who can tell me what this word means?" With student input, briefly define word and use the word in a sentence as an example.
Read the Story	
Post-Reading Discussion	*Review the book—show pictures and ask the following questions:* • Why is it hard for Gracie to keep up with Roo? • Do you think Gracie and Roo are having fun playing with each other? Why/why not? • Why do you think Roo was always the teacher? How do you think that made Roo feel? • Why doesn't Roo go to school with Gracie? How did that make Gracie feel? • Why does Gracie become the teacher when they play school? • Why do you think Gracie doesn't want to play school anymore? How does that make Roo feel? • How did Roo make Gracie feel in front of Sarah? • Why does Gracie tell Sarah she doesn't know Roo? How do you think that made Roo feel? • Why is Gracie suddenly not hungry? • Why does Gracie change her mind about telling Sarah who Roo is? • When they play school with Roo being the teacher again, how do you think it made Roo feel?

(continued)

From *Classroom Bullying Prevention, Pre-K–4th Grade: Children's Books, Lesson Plans, and Activities* by Melissa Allen Heath, Tina Taylor Dyches, and Mary Anne Prater. Santa Barbara, CA: Linworth. Copyright © 2013.

Lesson Plan 4.3
(Continued)

Extension Activities	Explain to the students that sometimes people feel sad because of things they can't help. For example, Gracie felt sad when Roo could not go to school with her, but Roo was too old. Sometimes people feel sad because of how others make them feel. We should not make others feel sad by pretending we don't know them, like Gracie did to her aunt Roo. Roo was a good friend and part of Gracie's family—her aunt. In this story Gracie sometimes makes Roo feel happy and sometimes she makes her feel sad. • Have students color one smiley face blue and one frowning face blue to represent Roo (point out that blue rhymes with Roo to help them remember). Color one smiley face red and one frowning face red to represent Gracie. Have them cut them out and tape a Popsicle/craft stick to the back. • Explain to the students that they are going to hold up a blue smiley face when Roo is happy in the story and a blue frowning face when she is sad. Read or retell the story modeling how to hold up the correct face for Roo. Repeat the sequence holding up the red faces (happy or sad) for Gracie. • Divide the class in half, asking one half of the students to hold up the red faces (Gracie) and the other half to hold up the blue faces (Roo).
Closure	Remind students that we should not make others feel sad, particularly by pretending we don't know them—like Gracie pretended not to know Roo in this story. Before we talk or act, we need to think about how the other person feels.

From *Classroom Bullying Prevention, Pre-K–4th Grade: Children's Books, Lesson Plans, and Activities* by Melissa Allen Heath, Tina Taylor Dyches, and Mary Anne Prater. Santa Barbara, CA: Linworth. Copyright © 2013.

Activity 4.3 *Keeping Up with Roo*

Directions: Color one pair of faces blue (for Roo) and one pair of faces red (for Gracie).

Cut out the circles and tape a Popsicle/craft stick to the back of each circle.

Book Summary 4.4
Thank You, Mr. Falker

Author: Patricia Polacco
Publisher: Philomel Books
Year: 1998
ISBN: 0-399-23166-8
ISBN 13: 978-0-399-23166-7
Number of Pages: 40 (no page numbers)
Reading Level: 4.1 (grade level)
Interest Level: K+

Synopsis: Tricia is excited to start school. She wants to learn to read. Her grandfather explains that knowledge learned from books is like tasting sweet honey. However, she has difficulty learning to read. She begins to feel different and dumb. After moving from Michigan to California, Trisha hopes to "start over." She hopes these students won't tease her because she has difficulty reading. But similar to her previous school, she is called names and ridiculed. Mr. Falker, her fifth-grade teacher, tells classmates that Trisha is a brilliant artist. This stops the in-class teasing, but bullying elsewhere escalates. One day Mr. Falker sends a student to the principal's office for taunting Tricia. Mr. Falker and the reading teacher work with Tricia, teaching her to read. In the end, we learn that this book is autobiographical.

Key Characteristics of Book's Characters and Bullying Situation	
Type of Characters	Humans
Bully's Gender, Age, & Race	Male, elementary age, Caucasian
Victim's Gender, Age, & Race	Female, elementary age, Caucasian
Bully's Age Compared to Victim	Same
Type of Bullying	Verbal (e.g., name calling, laughing at her), physical (e.g., jumping out at her, pulling her out of her hiding place)
Location of Bullying	Classroom, playground, lunchroom, stairwell, hallway, bathroom
Victim's Response to Bullying	Crying, hiding
Bully's Response to Bullying	Stops teasing in the classroom but continues elsewhere
Bystander's Response to Bullying	Joining in
Resolution	Teacher intervenes

From *Classroom Bullying Prevention, Pre-K–4th Grade: Children's Books, Lesson Plans, and Activities* by Melissa Allen Heath, Tina Taylor Dyches, and Mary Anne Prater. Santa Barbara, CA: Linworth. Copyright © 2013.

Lesson Plan 4.4
Thank You, Mr. Falker

Book: *Thank You, Mr. Falker* by Patricia Polacco (1998), Philomel Books

Reading Level: 4.1 (grade level)
Interest Level: K+

Lesson Objective(s): To teach that how we treat others affects how they feel. After listening to the story, students will identify four or five ways they can make others feel like they are tasting honey (good).

Materials: Samples of honey and vinegar in small containers for each child; crayons (to color bees); copies of bees (one bee for each student); copy of honey jar (bees and honey jar are included on the activity pages)

Pre-Reading Activities	• Tell students they are going to taste two different foods. Give each student two small containers—one with honey and one with vinegar. Ask them to dip their Popsicle/craft sticks into each and taste them. Ask students to provide words to describe what they tasted. Add words they don't provide (e.g., honey—sweet, yummy, sugary; vinegar—sour, bitter, yucky). Write them on the board in two different columns. • Tell students you are going to read a story about a girl who has some things happen to her that feel like eating honey and some things that feel like eating vinegar. • Read the title and show the book's front cover. Ask: "Who do you think Mr. Falker is? Who do you think is thanking him? Why?"
Key Vocabulary	**ladle, drizzled, knowledge, wiggling, twilight, fireflies, torture, wobbly, California, Michigan, two-tone, Plymouth, longed, abuzz, elegant, slick, brilliant, stumbling, fuzzy, plaid, fault, stairwell, mole, memorize, cunning, bravery, flicked, paragraph, odyssey, discovery, adventure** • Review key vocabulary: Inform students, "In this story you may hear a few words that may be unfamiliar to you." Either write words on the chalkboard/whiteboard or type and use word strips. • Show each word (one at a time) and ask, "Who can tell me what this word means?" With student input, briefly define word and use the word in a sentence as an example.
Read the Story	
Post-Reading Discussion	*Review the book—show pictures and ask the following questions:* • Why does the grandpa have the girl taste the honey? • What does he say honey is like? • Why did Tricia begin to feel dumb? Do you think that felt like tasting honey or vinegar? • Why did Tricia like being with her grandma? Do you think that felt like tasting honey or vinegar? • When the other children called Tricia dumb, do you think that felt like tasting honey or vinegar? • What did Mr. Falker call Tricia's drawings? Do you think that felt like tasting honey or vinegar?
Post-Reading Discussion	• When Eric and the other kids call her names, do you think that felt like tasting honey or vinegar? • How does Mr. Falker help Tricia? Do you think that felt like tasting honey or vinegar?

(continued)

Lesson Plan 4.4
(*Continued*)

Extension Activities	• Tell the students that each of us can make others feel like they are tasting honey or they are tasting vinegar. Explain that when we make others feel like they are tasting vinegar, then we are a bully and bullying will not be allowed in the school. • Ask students what different people did in the story that made Tricia feel like she was tasting honey or vinegar. Create a list on the board with headings: (1) Honey—being good at drawing, being told you are smart, being told you draw well. (2) Vinegar—feeling different, having hard time reading, feeling dumb, being called names, others laughing at you, hiding to avoid bully. • Explain that the students in the classroom are going to be like bees who make honey. As a class, generate a list of four or five positive things students will do to help others feel like they are tasting honey (e.g., say nice things, help others, tell an adult if someone is teasing). Write these statements on the honey jar (included on activity page). • Give each student a copy of a cut-out bee (included on activity page). Ask each student to color and write his/her name on their bee. Post the honey jar and the bees on the bulletin board.
Closure	Remind students of how honey and vinegar taste. Emphasize that in our classroom we will work on making others feel like they are tasting honey. Review the desired behaviors (listed on the honey jar). Explain that all the bees, including every one of us, make the honey sweet. Everyone needs to help.

Activity 4.4   *Thank You, Mr. Falker*

Crow Boy

Author: Taro Yashima
Publisher: Puffin Books
Year: 1955 (reprinted numerous times)
ISBN: 014050172X
ISBN 13: 978-0140501728
Number of Pages: 36 (not paginated)
Reading Level: 3.4
Interest Level: K+

Synopsis: This story takes place in Japan. A young boy, nicknamed Chibi (tiny boy), looked strange, dressed differently, and acted differently than other schoolchildren. Afraid of his teacher and classmates, he spent most of his time alone, not joining in with others. Classmates teased him, made faces, and called him "stupid" and "slowpoke." However, his new sixth-grade teacher took time to learn about his unique interests and talents. The teacher introduced Chibi in the school's talent show. All were amazed at Chibi's talent in mimicking crow calls. Appreciating this talent, all the children cried because they had treated Chibi so badly. Thereafter, everyone respectfully called him "Crow Boy," a name he liked.

Key Characteristics of Book's Characters and Bullying Situation	
Type of Characters	Humans
Bully's Gender, Age, & Race	Multiple bullies: males and females, all ages, Japanese
Victim's Gender, Age, & Race	Male, elementary-age, Japanese
Bully's Age Compared to Victim	Multiple bullies, all ages
Type of Bullying	Verbal and relational (name calling, making faces, excluding)
Location of Bullying	Classroom, playground
Victim's Response to Bullying	Ignoring, hiding, staying apart from others
Bully's Response to Bullying	Continued teasing and excluding victim
Bystander's Response to Bullying	Joined in with bullying
Resolution	New teacher befriends victim, spotlighting student in talent show (crow calls). Sorrowful, bullies cried, then showed respect for victim, calling him a name he appreciated—Crow Boy.

Lesson Plan 4.5
Crow Boy

Book: *Crow Boy* by Taro Yashima (1955—reprinted), Puffin Books

Reading Level: 3.4
Interest Level: K+

Lesson Objective(s): Teach appropriate ways to stop bullying and excluding—reinforcing take a stand, step in, and speak up. After listening to the story, students will discuss examples of ignoring, excluding, and teasing presented in the story. Then students will role-play ways to respond—take a stand, step in, and speak up—when faced with similar situations.

Materials: Role-Play scenarios (see activity pages following lesson plan), picture of crow (see activity pages following lesson plan)—copy one crow for each student, scissors (to cut out crow), black crayon for each child

Pre-Reading Activities	• Ask students if they have ever noticed someone being left out and not included during recess. • Show the book's cover and ask if the person on the cover looks similar to themselves. • State: "Today we are going to read a story that takes place in a faraway place, Japan. This boy (point to book's cover) looks different and acts differently than other children. Have you ever felt like you looked different or acted differently than other children? How did that make you feel?"
Key Vocabulary	**nickname, forlorn, grubs, trudging, imitate, attendance, proudly** • Review key vocabulary: Inform students, "In this story you may hear a few words that may be unfamiliar to you." Either write words on the chalkboard/whiteboard or type and use word strips. • Show each word (one at a time) and ask, "Who can tell me what this word means?" With student input, briefly define word and use the word in a sentence as an example.
Read the Story	
Post-Reading Discussion	*Review the book—show pictures and ask the following questions:* • What is different about Crow Boy? • Why does Crow Boy hide from others? • How does Mr. Isobe (the new teacher) learn interesting things about Crow Boy? • After Crow Boy imitated crow calls, why did the students and grownups cry? • Why did everyone stop calling him Chibi? • Do you think he preferred being called Chibi or Crow Boy?
Extension Activities	• Review the story's details, focusing on how classmates did not take a stand against bullying, how they did not step in when they saw others saying mean things to Crow Boy, and how they did not speak up to stop the bullying. Because no one spoke up for Crow Boy, this bullying continued for six years! The only person who took time to get to know Crow Boy was Mr. Isobe, the new sixth-grade teacher. • How could students get to know this boy? • What could students have done differently when they saw classmates making faces, calling Crow Boy stupid, and not including him in recess games or classroom activities?

(continued)

Lesson Plan 4.5
(Continued)

Extension Activities	• Teach students the three steps: (1) **TAKE A STAND.** This means thinking about the harm bullying causes, and deciding that bullying must be stopped. (2) Have the courage to **STEP IN**, rather than turn away and ignore what is happening. (3) **SPEAK UP** and say STOP IT! This takes courage. Sometimes having a few friends join us in saying STOP IT helps us feel supported. We are not alone. Many students want bullying to STOP. • Role-play the scenarios (activity page following lesson plan). Take time to discuss how students feel about bullying. • Hand out the crow picture to each student (activity page following scenarios). Ask students to color their crow (black); cut out their crow, leaving the wording on the bottom so that the crows can be linked together; then tape the crows end-to-end, forming a long strand of crows. Display the crows on a high perch above the bulletin board, windows, or high on the wall—similar to birds perched on high electrical wires.
Closure	• Review the three steps, "Take a stand, step in, and speak up." • Remind students that you will watch them to make sure they are using these three steps to stop bullying. The classroom flock of crows will be a visual reminder to "take a stand, step in, and speak up."

From *Classroom Bullying Prevention, Pre-K–4th Grade: Children's Books, Lesson Plans, and Activities* by Melissa Allen Heath, Tina Taylor Dyches, and Mary Anne Prater. Santa Barbara, CA: Linworth. Copyright © 2013.

Role-Play Scenarios

Read each scenario and then invite students to play a part and act out the role-play. Ask all students to join in with the words "STOP it" (included in each role-play).

(1) Leo is a new student in our school. He has cerebral palsy. It is hard for him to control his legs and arms, so he walks and moves in jerking motions. Julie and her three friends are pointing a finger at Leo and laughing because of how he walks. Leo is very sad and is trying to ignore the girls.

Take a stand: Their pointing fingers and laughter makes me feel sad. I know this is not kind. I do NOT like how I feel and how this hurts Leo's feelings.

Step in: I do not walk away and pretend I don't see what is happening. I walk up to where the girls are standing.

Speak up: I speak up in a strong voice, "**STOP it—STOP** making fun of Leo."

(2) Milo was in a car accident when he was four years old. Because of the accident, Milo has many scars on his face and arms. Several boys in Milo's class call him "Scarface." Milo is shy and has not told his teacher or parents about the teasing. Today it is school picture day. The boys are especially mean today. Milo does not want to have his picture taken. It is recess and we are playing a game of softball. Milo is on the team with the mean boys. I hear the boys call Milo "Scarface." This makes Milo cover his face and step back from everyone.

Take a stand: This makes me feel angry at the boys. This is not right. I talk to a couple of other kids on my team. They agree that Milo deserves better than this.

Step in: We walk up to where the boys are calling Milo "Scarface."

Speak up: We speak up in a strong voice, "**STOP** it." Then we ask Milo to play on our team.

(3) Rashonda was born with spina bifida. Her backbone did not cover and protect nerves that send messages from her brain to her legs. She is in a wheelchair because she cannot walk. At recess when everyone runs out to the playground, Rashonda trails far behind. When we are playing tag, many of the students refuse to include Rashonda. This happens almost every day.

Take a stand: I see Rashonda left out when we are playing tag. I talk to my two best friends about this. We all agree it is not right and we need to include Rashonda.

Step in: The recess bell rings. My two friends and I stand by Rashonda.

Speak up: A couple of boys and girls come up to Rashonda, saying she cannot play tag. My friends and I speak up in a strong voice, "**STOP** it." Then we ask Rashonda to play four-square with us (a ball bouncing game).

Take a stand

Step in

Speak up

Appendix A

Recommended Resources

Additional Recommended Children's Books

Carson, J., & Treatner, M. (2005). *Stop Teasing Taylor!* San Anselmo, CA: Treasure Bay. ISBN: 978-1-891327-62-9, 48 pages

In this "We Both Read" book, young Otis is not sure what to do when his friend Taylor is teased because of what he is wearing. Taylor gets the courage to tell the bullies to stop. The teacher encouraged the students to notice good things about each other.

Cook, J. (2009). *Bully B.E.A.N.S.* Chattanooga, TN: National Center for Youth Issues. ISBN: 1931636494

Core message: Bystanders have power to stop bullying (grades pre-K–3). Also available: *Bully BEANS Activity and Idea Book* (Cook, 2010).

Forler, N. (2009). *Bird Child*. Plattsburg, NY: Tundra Books. ISBN: 978-0887768941; 32 pages

In defense of a new student, Eliza stands up to the schoolyard bullies. Others join in creating a strong opposition to the bullies. The bullies, having lost their power, leave the victim to her supportive allies. This story feels genuine and provides a good example of bystander power. Additionally, the artwork is especially beautiful.

Ludwig, T., & Gustavson, A. (2006). *Just Kidding*. Berkeley, CA: Tricycle Press.

D.J. feels like a loser because he is teased by Vince. Vince claims his teasing is just a joke. D.J.'s dad helps him learn strategies for dealing with teasing. The classroom teacher and school counselor also help.

Millman, D., & Bruce, T. T. (1991). *Secret of the Peaceful Warrior*. Tiburon, CA: Starseed Press. ISBN: 9780915811236; 32 pages

New to the neighborhood, Danny is confronted by a bully. He learns a secret from an old man named Socrates about how to overcome his fears—not by fighting or running away but by using the secret of the peaceful warrior. This story demonstrates the potential for adults to assist those who are bullied. The victim is not alone.

Pendziwol, J. E., & Gourbault, M. (2007). *Tale of Sir Dragon*. Toronto, ON: Kids Can Press. ISBN: 978-1554531363; 32 pages

During activities at camp, a young girl's dragon friend is bullied for being too big, tall, and green to play "knights" with them. The queen and king help the dragon and teach the children to play together. The potential of bystanders to support victims is emphasized. In addition to the story, the book contains additional activities that could be implemented in classrooms.

Russo, M. (2010). *A Very Big Bunny*. New York, NY: Schwartz and Wade. ISBN: 9780375844638; 40 pages

Amelia is a very tall bunny who is routinely excluded. Her classmates say that her feet are too big and that she is too tall to play the recess games. Each day, she stands alone. Her loneliness is disrupted by a very small bunny who moves into the neighborhood. This story demonstrates the painful feelings of being left out and also demonstrates how a new friendship can end that isolation.

Picture Books to Help Children Understand Emotions

Freymann, S., & Elffers, J. (1999). *How Are You Peeling? Foods with Moods*. New York, NY: Scholastic. ISBN: 978-0439104319; 48 pages

This book uses vegetables to demonstrate emotional expressions and feelings. This is a comfortable way to initiate conversations about emotions. After reading the book, have children identify their favorite pictures and consider situations or events that may have precipitated such feelings. Follow up with a discussion about what we might say or do to comfort someone in this situation.

McCloud, C. (2006). *Have You Filled a Bucket Today? A Guide to Daily Happiness for Kids.* Northville, MI: Nelson Publishing and Marketing. ISBN: 0978507517; 32 pages

This book encourages children to be thoughtful of others' feelings. The bucket metaphor illustrates the link between our kind words and acts of service and others' happiness—and subsequently our own happiness. Children are encouraged to help fill others' buckets. After reading the story, place a bucket in the classroom or school's office area, reminding children about the importance of "filling buckets." Based on practitioners' feedback, this book is highly effective in boosting thoughtfulness and classroom happiness.

Articles Describing Bibliotherapy for Children

Gregory, K. E., & Vessey, J. A. (2004). Bibliotherapy: A strategy to help students with bullying. *The Journal of School Nursing,* 20, 127–133.

Heath, M. A., Sheen, D., Leavy, D., Young, E. L., & Money, K. (2005). Bibliotherapy: A resource to facilitate emotional healing and growth. *School Psychology International,* 26, 563–580.

Prater, M. A., Johnstun, M. L., Dyches, T. T., & Johnstun, M. R. (2006). Using children's books as bibliotherpay for at-risk students: A guide for teachers. *Preventing School Failure,* 50, 5–13.

Rozalski, M., Stewart, A., & Miller, J. (2010, Fall). Bibliotherapy: Helping children cope with life's challenges. *Kappa Delta Pi Record,* 47, 33–37. Retrieved from http://www.kdp.org/publications/pdf/record/fall10/Record_Fall_2010_Rozalski.pdf

Professional Books

Beane, A. L. (2005). *The Bully-Free Classroom: Over 100 Tips and Strategies for Teachers K–8.* Minneapolis, MN: Free Spirit. ISBN: 101575421941; 166 pages

Strategies included in the book are practical and easy to implement. Suggested strategies focus on building students' interpersonal skills and creating positive supportive classrooms. Beane recommends classroom learning activities (e.g., games, discussions, and writing activities). The book also includes a resource list with recommended children's books (K–8th grade). Topics include bullying, friendship, conflict resolution, and acceptance/inclusion of peers.

Black, S. T. (2008). *Classroom Guidance Games.* Chapin, SC: YouthLight. ISBN: 1598500023; 261 pages

Contains 50 activities/games for Pre-K–6th-grade classrooms. Minimal preparation is required to implement the lesson plans. Lesson plans are well organized and include clear descriptions of activities with reproducible cards and worksheets. Games take less than 30 minutes of classroom time and are centered on a variety of important social skills—including bully prevention; friendship; study skills; anger management; emotions; politeness, manners, and respect; cooperation; career exploration; and self-esteem. The book also includes sample letters to inform parents about classroom guidance topics.

Coloroso, B. (2008). *The Bully, the Bullied, and the Bystander.* New York, NY: Harper. ISBN: 0061744603; 272 pages

Coloroso's major focus is on strengthening bystanders, encouraging students to speak up and take an active stance against bullying. This book clearly describes the multiple roles students play: either as victims, bullies, or passive enabling bystanders. Coloroso emphasizes the importance of building bystander power, encouraging students to speaking up and take action to stop bullying. Although geared primarily to teachers, this book is also a great resource for parents and all professionals who work with children.

Henkin, R. (2005). *Confronting Bullying: Literacy as a Tool for Character Education.* Portsmouth, NH: Heinemann. ISBN: 0325004137; 112 pages

Outlines a comprehensive program utilizing children's literature to tackle bullying and teach pro-social skills. Includes extensive booklist.

McNamara, B. E., & McNamara, F. J. (1997). *Keys to Dealing with Bullies.* New York, NY: Barron's Educational Series. ISBN: 0764101633; 138 pages

In addition to strategies for dealing with bullies, this book contains an appendix with listed fiction and nonfiction books on the topic of bullying. Authors recommend reading books to initiate discussion.

Moulton, E., *Confronting Bullying: Searching for Strategies in Children's Literature*, PhD diss., Brigham Young University. Retrieved from http://edts523naz.wikispaces.com/file/view/etd2991.pdf

Moulton's thesis is available online (PDF file). She analyzed 29 children's bully-themed picture books published between 2004 and 2009. She includes tables in Appendix C, pages 96–105. These tables describe the identified books in regard to descriptions of bullies and victims, types of bullying, reactions of bystanders, and resolutions of bullying situation. Additionally, she describes awards won and *The Horn Book* ratings (library journal that reviews books for quality and content).

Prater, M. A., & Dyches, T. T. (2008). *Teaching about Disabilities through Children's Literature*. Westport, CT: Libraries Unlimited. ISBN: 9781591585411; 131 pages

This resource guides educators in sharing children's literature to help children learn about disabilities. Highlighting elements of quality literature (picture books through young adult novels), the authors offer insights regarding literature's ability to help children gain an awareness of disabilities, knowledge of disabilities and of challenges facing those affected by disabilities, and an understanding of social issues affecting those with disabilities. Optimally, quality literature offers children an opportunity to emotionally engage and think on a deeper level about themselves and their attitudes and perceptions regarding others who are different. These deeper feelings help children challenge and change previous tendencies to disregard, marginalize, or bully those who may look or act differently. Other sections of the book include an annotated bibliography of books that include characters with disabilities; five lesson plans, offering a template for using children's literature to teach about disabilities; unit plans for junior and high school students; a section of activities and reproducible worksheets; and an appendix with additional resources.

Ragona, S., & Pentel, K. (2008). *Eliminating Bullying in Grades PK–3*. Chapin, SC: YouthLight. ISBN: 1889636681; 136 pages

Contains 10 easy-to-implement lesson plans that encourage victims and bystanders to get involved and to take a stand against bullying. Stories and coping strategies are centered on animals. Children will enjoy these fun activities. Includes worksheets and sample letters to parents.

Websites

http://www.anti-bullyingalliance.org.uk/downloads/pdf/fictionlist2007.pdf

Anti-Bullying Alliance promotes bibliotherapy, suggesting books to strengthen children's coping skills. This website lists brief summaries of over 50 bully-themed children's books, including each book's identifying information (e.g., authors and publication information).

http://www.best-childrens-books.com/childrens-books-about-bullying.html

Best Children's Books offers a list of bully-themed children's books. Indicating a rough estimate of quality, this site specifies the number of respected book lists that include each book.

http://www.dps.mo.gov/homelandsecurity/safeschools/documents/Discussion%20Activities%20for%20School%20Communities .pdf

This website, National School Safety Center, is an excellent resource for bully-themed training materials, fact sheets, and handouts. The site includes *Bullying in Schools: Fighting the Bully Battle* (Quiroz, Arnette, & Stephens, 2006). This 14-page booklet for parents, schools, and communities identifies strategies to decrease bullying.

http://www.schoolsafety.us/free-resources/bullying-in-schools-discussion-activities-for-school-communities

National School Safety Center's *Bullying in Schools: Fighting the Bully Battle: Discussion Activities for School Communities* includes a teacher lesson plan with 24 pages of classroom training materials.

http://www.jimwrightonline.com/pdfdocs/bully/bystander.pdf

Intervention Central contains Jim Wright's (2003) four-page article "Bystanders: Turning Onlookers into Bully-Prevention Agents." This resource offers classroom discussion points and includes role-plays and activities to involve students in taking a stand against bullying. These activities reinforce the essential concept of strengthening bystander support to deter bullying.

http://www.sprc.org/library/Suicide_Bullying_Issue_Brief.pdf

Suicide Prevention Resource Center (SPRC, 2011) published an eight-page handout on suicide and bullying titled "Suicide and Bullying: Issue Brief." Included in this handout are suggestions and recommendations for decreasing bullying in schools. The handout also included suicide risk factors linked to bullying, particularly identifying increased risk for lesbian, gay, bisexual, and transgender (LGBT) youth.

http://www.abilitypath.org/areas-of-development/learning--schools/bullying/articles/walk-a-mile-in-their-shoes.pdf

Walk a Mile in Their Shoes: Bullying and the Child with Special Needs. This 58-page booklet is produced by AbilityPath.org.

http://www.operationrespect.org/pdf/guide.pdf

Don't Laugh at Me: Teachers Guide: Grades 2-5: Creating a Ridicule-Free Classroom.

This 102-page booklet was produced by Operation Respect and includes classroom lesson plans and associated activities related to the following topics: expressing feelings; caring, compassion, and cooperation; resolving conflict creatively; and celebrating diversity.

PICTURES

(1) Take a stand

I **take a stand** against bullying.

From *Classroom Bullying Prevention, Pre-K–4th Grade: Children's Books, Lesson Plans, and Activities* by Melissa Allen Heath, Tina Taylor Dyches, and Mary Anne Prater. Santa Barbara, CA: Linworth. Copyright © 2013.

(2) Step in

I **step in** and protect those who are bullied.

(3) Speak up

I **speak up** when I see bullying.

Appendix B

Lesson Plan Vocabulary Words

Chapter 3 Books	Vocabulary Words
The Bully Blockers Club	tattletale, karate chop, prickled, smack, allergic, grownups, clubs, bullying
Chrysanthemum	precious, priceless, fascinating, winsome, miserably, jealous, begrudging, discontented, jaundiced, indescribable, wilted, dreadful, humorous
Feathers	gossip, rumor, rabbi, jest, justice, amends, crime, accused, careless, excused, humor, snatch, weary, scattered, cruel, rind
Howard B. Wigglebottom Learns about Bullies	"little voice in his head," brave, bold, "fist-punching," "name-calling," "worm-whomping," "tongue-wagging," "foot-stomping," tattletale, snitch, cloak, invisible, twirl, hurl, outer space, stubby legged, amazement, drifted, imagination
I Get So Hungry	gobble, checkups, deserve, diet, thinner, fried food
I Like Who I Am	Mohawk, ignore, creation, blush, clenched, pow wow, culture, gaping, taunted, demonstration
The Juice Box Bully	snarled, growled, spitefully, shrieked, demanded, bystander
Leave Me Alone	miserable, "pass you by," downhearted, sobbing, whiskers, wilt, chat, habit, giant, casts, firm, enemy, sneered, snarled, stomped
Lucy and the Bully	accident, model, jealous, artistic, crumpled, wailed
Nobody Knew What to Do: A Story about Bullying	behave, "picking on," bully, tattle/report, narrator
The Recess Queen	smoosh, lollapaloosh, kitz and kajammer, puny, loony, dared, gaped, whizzed
Say Something	hero, "picked on," teased, cafeteria, disappear
Stand Tall, Molly Lou Melon	confident, bullfrog, boa constrictor, "fumble fingered," "shrimpo," glee, worth
Yoon and the Jade Bracelet	disappointment, jade, gem, tricked, trickster, etched, symbol, wisdom, shame, courage
Don't Laugh at Me	geek, braces, beggar, stare, deaf, blind

Chapter 4 Books	Vocabulary Words
Be Good to Eddie Lee	lonesome, waddled, ignored, kingfisher, hatched, whopper, salamander, quiver, water lilies, tadpoles, reflection
My Sister, Alicia Mae	astronaut, polka dots, notices, caboose, "sharp memory," forever, annoy
Keeping Up with Roo	swoop, quiver, flung, pumping, version, "Stars and Stripes Forever," wake, adventures, tart, corral, sprained, water skeeters, apple crates, willow switch, crossroads, overalls, experimenting, fluttered, abandoned, May pole, drizzled, reruns
Thank You, Mr. Falker	ladle, drizzled, knowledge, wiggling, twilight, fireflies, torture, wobbly, California, Michigan, two-tone, Plymouth, longed, abuzz, elegant, slick, brilliant, stumbling, fuzzy, plaid, fault, stairwell, mole, memorize, cunning, bravery, flicked, paragraph, odyssey, discovery, adventure
Crow Boy	nickname, forlorn, grubs, trudging, imitate, attendance, proudly

References

Berger, K. S. (2007). Update on bullying at school: Science forgotten? *Developmental Review, 27*(1), 90–126.

Cobb, B., Sample, P. L., Alwell, M., & Johns, N. R. (2006). Cognitive-behavioral interventions, dropout, and youth with disabilities. *Remedial and Special Education, 27*(5), 259–275. doi: 10.1177/07419325060270050201

Cohen, J. A., Mannarino, A. P., & Deblinger, E. (2006). *Treating Trauma and Traumatic Grief in Children and Adolescents.* New York, NY: Guilford.

Coie, J. D. (2004). The impact of negative social experiences on the development of antisocial behavior. In J. B. Kupersmidt & K. A. Dodge (Eds.), *Children's Peer Relations from Development to Intervention* (pp. 209–222). Washington, DC: American Psychological Association.

Coloroso, B. (2008). *The Bully, the Bullied, and the Bystander.* New York, NY: Harper.

Coville, B. (1990, Fall). Magic mirrors. *Bookmark, 49*(1), 35–36.

Davidson, L. M., & Demaray, M. K. (2007). Social support as a moderator between victimization and internalizing–externalizing distress from bullying. *School Psychology Review, 36,* 383–405.

Davis, S., & Davis, J. (2007). *Schools Where Everyone Belongs: Practical Strategies for Reducing Bullying* (2nd ed.). Champaign, IL: Research.

Entenmen, J., Murnen, T. J., & Hendricks, C. (2005). Victims, bullies, and bystanders in K–3 literature. *Reading Teacher, 59*(4), 352–364.

Forgan, J. W. (2002). Using bibliotherapy to teach problem solving. *Intervention in School and Clinic, 38*(2), 75–82.

Gregory, K. E., & Vessey, J. A. (2004). Bibliotherapy: A strategy to help students with bullying. *Journal of School Nursing, 20*(3), 127–133.

Heath, M. A., Moulton, E., Dyches, T. T., Prater, M. A., & Brown, A. (2011). Strengthening elementary school bully prevention with bibliotherapy. *Communique, 39*(8), 12–14.

Heath, M. A., Sheen, D., Leavy, D., Young, E. L., & Money, K. (2005). Bibliotherapy: A resource to facilitate emotional healing and growth. *School Psychology International, 26,* 563–580.

Henkin, R. (2005). *Confronting Bullying: Literacy as a Tool for Character Education.* Portsmouth, NH: Heinemann.

Hillsberg, C., & Spak, H. (2006). Young adult literature as the centerpiece of an anti-bullying program in middle school. *Middle School Journal, 38*(2), 23–28.

Hoover, J., & Stenhjem, P. (2003, December). Bullying and teasing of youth with disabilities: Creating positive school environments for effective inclusion. *National Center on Secondary Education and Transition: Issue Brief, 2*(3), 1–6. Retrieved from http://www.ncset.org/publications/issue/NCSETIssueBrief_2.3.pdf.

Johnson, B. (2008). Teacher–student relationships which promote resilience at school: A micro-level analysis of students' views. *British Journal of Guidance and Counselling, 36*(4), 385–398. doi: 10.1080/03069880802364528

Merrell, K. W., Gueldern, B. A., Ross, S. W., & Isava, D. M. (2008). How effective are school bullying intervention programs? A meta-analysis of intervention research. *School Psychology Quarterly, 23*(1), 26–42.

Moulton, E., Heath, M. A., Prater, M. A., & Dyches, T. T. (2011). Portrayals of bullying in children's picture books and implications for bibliotherapy. *Reading Horizons, 51*(2), 119–148.

Nansel, T. R., Craig, W., Overpeck, M. D., Saluja, G., & Ruan, W. J. (2004). Cross-national consistency in the relationship between bullying behaviors & psychosocial adjustment. *Archives of Pediatrics & Adolescent Medicine, 158*(8), 730–736.

Nansel, T. R., Overpeck, M. D., Haynie, D. L., Ruan, W. J., & Scheidt, P. C. (2003). Relationships between bullying and violence among US youth. *Archives of Pediatrics & Adolescent Medicine, 157*(4), 348–353.

Oliver, R. L., Young, T. A., & LaSalle, S. M. (1994). Early lessons in bullying and victimization: The help and hindrance of children's literature. *School Counselor, 42*(2), 137–146.

Olweus, D. (1993). *Bullying at School: What We Know and What We Can Do.* Cambridge, MA: Blackwell Publishers.

Parault, S. J., Davis, H. A., & Pelligrini, A. D. (2007). The social contexts of bullying and victimization. *Journal of Early Adolescence, 27*(2), 145–174.

Prater, M. A., Johnstun, M. L., Dyches, T. T., & Johnstun, M. R. (2006). Using children's books as bibliotherapy for at-risk students: A guide for teachers. *Preventing School Failure, 50*(4), 5–13.

Rapee, R. M., Abbott, M. J., & Lyneham, H. J. (2006). Bibliotherapy for children with anxiety disorders using written materials for parents: A randomized controlled trial. *Journal of Consulting and Clinical Psychology, 74*(3), 436–444.

Reading Rockets. (n.d.). *Directed reading and thinking activity.* Arlington, VA: WETA. Retrieved from http://www.readingrockets.org/strategies/drta/.

Rose, C. A., Monda-Amaya, L. E., & Espelage, D. L. (2011). Bullying perpetration and victimization in special education: A review of the literature. *Remedial and Special Education, 32*(2), 114–130.

Shechtman, Z. (1999). Bibliotherapy: An indirect approach to treatment of childhood aggression. *Child Psychiatry & Human Development, 30*(1), 39–53.

Shechtman, Z. (2000). An innovative intervention for treatment of child and adolescent aggression: An outcome study. *Psychology in the Schools, 37*(2), 157–167.

Shechtman, Z. (2006). The contribution of bibliotherapy to the counseling of aggressive boys. *Psychotherapy Research, 16*(5), 631–636.

Sipe, L. R. (2008). *Storytime: Young Children's Literary Understanding in the Classroom.* New York, NY: Teachers College Press.

Sprague, J. R., & Walker, H. M. (2005). *Safe and Healthy Schools: Practical Intervention Strategies.* New York: Guilford.

Stice, E., Rohde, P., Seeley, J. R., & Gau, J. M. (2008). Brief cognitive-behavioral depression prevention program for high-risk adolescents outperforms two alternative interventions: A randomized efficacy trial. *Journal of Consulting Clinical Psychology, 76*(4), 595–606.

Teglasi, H., Rahill, S., & Rothman, L. (2007). A story-guided peer group intervention for reducing bullying and victimization in schools. In J. E. Zins, M. J. Elias, & C. A. Maher (Eds.), *Bullying, Victimization, and Peer Harassment: A Handbook of Prevention and Intervention* (pp. 219–237). New York, NY: Haworth Press.

United States Department of Education. (2010, August 26). *Guidance Targeting Harassment Outlines Local and Federal Responsibility.* Washington, DC: Author. Retrieved from http://www.ed.gov/news/press-releases/guidance-targeting-harassment-outlines-local-and-federal-responsibility.

United States Department of Education, National Center for Education Statistics. (2010). *The Condition of Education: Participation in Education, Table A-7-2, Percentage Distribution of Students Ages 6–21 Served under the Individuals with Disabilities Education Act (IDEA), Part B, by Educational Environment and Type of Disability: Selected School Years, 1990–91 through 2008–09.* Washington DC: Author. Retrieved from http://nces.ed.gov/programs/coe/tables/table-cwd-2.asp.

Willard, N. E. (2007). The authority and responsibility of school officials in responding to cyberbullying. *Journal of Adolescent Health, 41*(6), S64–S65. doi: 10.1016/j.jadohealth.2007.08.013

Index

About the Authors

MELISSA ALLEN HEATH, PhD, is an associate professor in Brigham Young University's Department of Counseling Psychology and Special Education. She co-authored *School-Based Crisis Intervention* and has authored numerous articles that support bibliotherapy as an effective intervention to address children's social-emotional needs. Dr. Heath holds a doctorate in school psychology from Texas A&M University, College Station, Texas.

TINA TAYLOR DYCHES, EdD, is an associate professor in the Department of Counseling Psychology and Special Education at Brigham Young University. Dr. Dyches has worked in the field of helping individuals with disabilities and their families for over 25 years, as a special educator, professor, and consultant. Dr. Dyches has written several articles and two books about using children's literature that includes characters with disabilities. She is one of the founders of the Dolly Gray Children's Literature Award, which recognizes high-quality children's books that portray characters with developmental disabilities.

MARY ANNE PRATER, PhD, is a professor in the Department of Counseling Psychology and Special Education at Brigham Young University. She has taught in Utah, Illinois, Hawaii, and Alaska. Dr. Prater's areas of expertise include instructional strategies for students with mild to moderate disabilities, special education teacher preparation, and the portrayal of disabilities in children's literature. She is a co-founder of the Dolly Gray Children's Literature Award. This is her seventh book.

Edwards Brothers Malloy
Thorofare, NJ USA
November 1, 2013